REFERENCE SERVICE

LIBRARY MANAGEMENT SERIES

Number one: Planning-Programming-Budgeting System: Implications for Library Management

Number two: Legal Reference Collections for Non-Law Libraries: A Survey of Holdings in the Academic Community

Number three: Library Budgeting: Critical Challenges for the Future

Number four: Emerging Trends in Library Organization: What Influences Change

Number five: Serials Collection Development: Choices and Strategies

Number six: Reference Service: A Perspective

REFERENCE SERVICE: A PERSPECTIVE

edited by
Sul H. Lee

Dean, University Libraries
Professor of Bibliography
The University of Oklahoma

THE PIERIAN PRESS
1983

Library of Congress Catalog Card Number 83-60917
ISBN 0-87650-150-1

Copyright © 1983, The Pierian Press
All Rights Reserved

THE PIERIAN PRESS
P.O. Box 1808
Ann Arbor, MI. 48106

For Melissa

Contents

Introduction ix

The Personal Touch: A Brief Overview of Reference
       Services in American Libraries 1
Charles A. Bunge

The Role of Reference Service in the Mission of the
       Academic Library 17
Herbert White

Reference and the Other Technical Services in a Large
       University Library 31
William Miller

Professional Attitudes, Productive Roles: Roads to
       Achievement 47
Keith M. Cottam

The Widening Gyre: Resource Sharing and Its Impact
       on Reference Services 63
Sheila Dowd

The Impact of User Education and Computer Searching
       Programs on Reference Services 79
Kathleen Gunning

Evaluation and Measurement of Reference Service:
       Problems, Approaches, and Potential 89
Maurice P. Marchant

"Fees or Free" 99
Anne K. Beaubien

Bibliography 113
Rodney M. Hersberger

Index 125

Introduction

Reference service is an activity common to all libraries. On October 7 and 8, 1982 the University of Oklahoma Libraries and the University of Oklahoma Foundation sponsored a conference to examine the dynamics of reference services in a changing environment. The conference in Oklahoma City was attended by more than 80 librarians from throughout the U.S. and Canada. A diverse group of speakers stimulated the audience and invited a lively discussion about reference services.

One might well inquire about the need to examine reference services. Surely, the argument might go, we all know how to provide reference services since libraries offer so much in the way of reference services. The speakers and audience took issue without complacency about the provision of reference services and challenged each other to take a measured and critical look at just how well we are serving our public at the reference desk.

The conference sought a definition of reference service and asked why we provide it. One speaker addressed the measurement of reference services while another discussed professional qualifications for persons offering that service. Others reviewed the impact of collection development, resource sharing, user education and technology on reference. The conference concluded with a provocative examination and discussion of fee based reference services.

The papers presented at the conference are included and published here. Charles H. Bunge wrote a lead paper for this volume which was not presented at the conference: "The Personal Touch: A Brief Overview of the Development of Reference Services in American Libraries." There were seven formal papers prepared for and delivered at the conference: 1) Herbert White (Dean, School of Library and Information Science, Indiana University) "The Role of Reference Service in the Mission of the Academic Library"; 2) William Miller (Head of Reference, Michigan State University Libraries) "Reference and the Other Technical Services in a Large

University Library"; 3) Keith Cottam (Acting Director, Vanderbilt University Library) "Professional Attitudes, Productive Roles: Roads to Achievement"; 4) Sheila Dowd (Assistant University Librarian for Collection Development and Reference Services, University of California Libraries, Berkeley) "The Widening Gyre: Resource Sharing and Its Impact on Reference Services"; 5) Kathleen Gunning (Head of Reference, University of Houston Libraries) "The Impact of User Education and Computer Searching Programs on Reference Services"; 6) Maurice Marchant (Professor, School of Library and Information Sciences, Brigham Young University) "Evaluation and Measurement of Reference Service: Problems, Approaches, and Potential"; 7) Anne Beaubien (Director, Michigan Information Transfer Source, University of Michigan Libraries) "Fees or Free." Also, Rodney Hersberger (Assistant to the Dean for Administrative Services, University of Oklahoma Libraries) prepared the "Bibliography."

While it is valuable to share the conference papers with the academic library community, it is difficult to convey the sense of conference participation through the more sterile pages of a monograph. Hopefully, however, the reader, too, can be stimulated by the papers and find additional source material through the bibliography.

I am pleased to acknowledge my debt to Mr. Ron D. Burton, Executive Director of the University of Oklahoma Foundation for the generous support he and the Foundation provided the conference. Mr. Burton is an enthusiastic supporter of the University of Oklahoma Libraries and has contributed many times to our program.

Sul H. Lee
Norman, Oklahoma
January 7, 1983

THE PERSONAL TOUCH

A Brief Overview of the Development of Reference Services in American Libraries[1]

Charles A. Bunge

Definition and Theory

The Reference and Adult Services Division of ALA has defined reference service as personal assistance provided to users in the pursuit of information.[1] Reference service can be distinguished from other library activities or services by its high degree of personal interaction between library staff members and library users, its provision of services to specific individual users or identified small groups of users, and the knowledge of the information needs of the users that the reference librarian has at the time the service is provided.

The theory of reference service has been discussed in the literature since its early days. Many of these discussions have treated the appropriate level of service to be provided by the reference librarian. They have set out what have been called the "conservative," "moderate," and "liberal" theories or philosophies of service, depending on the emphasis given to teaching the patrons to help themselves or to providing the information itself in answer to questions. [2; 3, pp. 6–13]

Other theoretical approaches to reference services have concentrated on the reference process, attempting to break it down into its component parts and to show the relationships between the parts. Jesse Shera and Alan Rees took this approach in discussing how computers might affect reference services, and the present author used the same approach in discussing the impact of library cooperation. [4; 5; 6] Jahoda and Katz have summarized a number of such studies. [7; 8, Vol. II, pp. 67--94]

Robert Wagers, in an excellent paper on reference theory, argues that setting up dichotomies between such functions of reference service as instruction and information providing is not a fruitful way to advance the development of theory or service.[9] He encourages inquiring into the relationships among the various elements of reference service. Along a similar line, Margaret E. Monroe, in a recent theoretical paper, identifies the important elements in historic and emerging patterns of reference and adult services.[10] For Monroe, the variables that should be related in a theory of reader services are the needs of the publics served, the activities performed (e.g., collection development, literature searches, bibliography preparation, presentations to small groups, question answering, etc.), and the functions served. Adding to formulations by Samuel Rothstein, Monroe identifies these functions as information (finding needed information for the user or assisting in finding such information), instruction (helping users learn the skills they need to find and use materials and information), guidance (assisting users to choose materials appropriate to their educational, informational, or recreational needs), and stimulation (making potential users aware of the relevance of library services to their needs). This formulation will provide the framework for the later sections of this paper.

Historical Overview

Louis Kaplan and Rothstein were able to find isolated examples of the provision of user assistance from the 1820s forward by such leaders as George Watterson, William F. Poole, and Charles Jewett. [11, pp. 1–2; 12, p. 20] However, such assistance as a systematically provided service had its real beginnings in American librarianship in the last quarter of the nineteenth century.[2] Most historians of reference service find it convenient to begin with an 1876 paper by Samuel Swett Green, entitled "The Desirableness of Establishing Personal Intercourse and Relations Between Librarians and Readers in Popular Libraries."[3] Until this time, the predominant view of the function of library service emphasized the acquisition and organization of library materials, and library clientele were expected to use the materials independently. Green, on the other hand, pointed out that library users were unskilled in the use of the catalog to find materials and lacked the knowledge necessary to select the material appropriate to their needs. Personal assistance to such users, said Green, would be of benefit to them and would result in a more positive view of the library.

Green's ideas won widespread acceptance and support. By the 1890s, the term "reference work" was replacing the earlier terms, "aid to readers" and "assistance to readers." This was particularly true in public libraries, where, by the turn of the century, most larger libraries were employing identified reference staffs. The early years of the twentieth century saw the establishment of separate reference departments in public libraries, the acceptance of reference questions via telephone and correspondence, the extension of reference service to branches, and the differentiation of reference services by level of complexity and subject field. During the period between the two world wars, public libraries developed methods to deal with the greatly increased number of requests for assistance and began to apply specialized techniques to different types of requests. The "information desk," to deal with the multitude of directional and simple requests, "readers' advisory services," to assist readers in choosing materials for self-education and development, and the growth of subject specialist reference librarians and departments were all features of reference service that developed in the 1918 to 1940 period.

The development of special libraries in the early twentieth century, with their concept of amplified service, was fertile ground for the development of reference service concepts and techniques. Especially important in the period before World War I was the application of special librarianship to the field of legislative and municipal reference work. The basis of such work, and the example it held out to reference work elsewhere, was a detailed knowledge by the librarian of the information needs of the clientele, a thorough knowledge of information sources and a willingness to seek out needed information from any source, and an ability to synthesize or otherwise to prepare information for use by the client. During and following the first world war, reference work in business, industrial, and research libraries assumed increasing importance. By the 1940s the special librarian frequently offered the following services: answering of factual inquiries, preparation of bibliographies, scanning and referring incoming literature, preparation of abstracts and translations of literature, and doing literature searches.

Rothstein points out that the development of reference service was slower in college and university libraries than in public and special libraries.[12, pp. 34--38] This was due, at least in part, to the expectation that faculty members and students should be able to find their own materials and information and to the emphasis the scholarly community placed on collection development and subject access to materials through cataloging. By the turn of the century, in spite of the example of a well developed reference service established by Melvil Dewey at Columbia University, full-time reference staffs were not yet common in academic libraries. In the early decades of the century the relatively new state university libraries led the way in establishing reference services, and by the time of World War I, reference work was accepted as a necessary service in a university library. The years between the world wars saw a great increase in the number and variety of reference questions, the establishment of separate reference departments in many or most university libraries, and their assumption of such duties as special bibliographic and indexing projects and greatly expanded interlibrary loan work.

In the first half of the twentieth century, then, proponents of reference services achieved widespread agreement on the importance of such service, as well as the development of the basic concepts and methods of reference work. While different libraries and librarians used different mixes and emphases, Monroe's elements, especially the functions of instruction, guidance, and information, were present and ready to be elaborated and refined in the 1960s and 1970s.

Instruction in Library Use

From the time of Samuel Swett Green's ground breaking paper to the present, instruction in the use of the library and library materials has been an important facet of reference service.[4] The planners of the conference on which this volume is based recognized the importance of the instruction function by making it the subject of one of the following papers. Contemporaries of Green, both librarians and non-librarians such as university presidents, urged the importance of teaching library users about books and the bibliographic apparatus for their location and use. Throughout the first half of the century, there were frequent references in the literature of librarianship to the need for such instruction and to the nature and content of the programs that were instituted. After a period of debate in the 1960s between those who emphasized information and those who emphasized instruction as the legitimate role of reference service, there was a resurgence of interest in library instruction in the 1970s, leading to the establishment of the Library Instruction Round Table in ALA in 1977.

Instruction in library use has had its fullest development in school libraries. For several decades most school librarians and teachers have agreed on the importance of teaching skills in the use of libraries and library materials to elementary and secondary school students. Many states and individual school districts have adopted courses of study in library instruction to be integrated with other parts of the curriculum. Recent discussions and developments in the school library field have concentrated on teaching techniques and methods, strategies for obtaining the cooperation of classroom teachers, and the evaluation of instruction programs.

Public and special libraries have emphasized the information and guidance aspects of reference service so that, in the main, their library instruction programs have consisted of basic orientation to the library and to publicity regarding the library and its services. Over the years, there has been considerable discussion of the need for more extensive efforts, and there have been specific programs related to individual subject areas, user groups, or projects. However, these have not had much cumulative impact on services in either public or special libraries.

The most recent developments in library instruction have occurred in college and university libraries. Many of these developments occurred in the 1970s. They include the establishment in 1977 of the Bibliographic Instruction Section of the Association of College and Research Libraries (ACRL) and the issuance in 1977 by ACRL of "Guidelines for Bibliographic Instruction in Academic Libraries." [17]

Several important aspects of instruction in library use have been clarified and developed in the last decade in college and university libraries. First, the philosophy has been enunciated that knowledge and skill in the use of information resources has importance beyond that attached to succeeding in one's college or university career. Indeed, the learning of such skill is important preparation for a lifetime of information use, especially in the post-industrial society, and such learning is an important objective for the curriculum of the college or university as a whole.

"Library orientation," a term once used almost synonymously with library instruction, is now generally recognized as only the most basic aspect of library instruction, consisting of familiarizing users with the library's policies, procedures, and lay out. Library instruction (commonly referred to as "bibliographic instruction") is of three major types: the separate course, course or assignment-related instruction, and point-of-use or point-of-need instruction.

The separate course or set of learning experiences usually has a combination of content about the use of information and bibliographic tools in general and about the use of the specific library resources on the campus where it is offered. In recent years these courses have employed such techniques as computer-assisted instruction, workbooks, media presentations, and other individualized and programmed instruction. In course-related bibliographic instruction the librarian and the subject classroom teacher cooperate so that the librarian helps students learn about bibliographic methods and library resources as a part of the course and at a time when the students have a need for learning, in order to complete other course requirements.

Point-of-use library instruction involves the provision of instructional assistance at the time and place where a library user encounters a problem. Perhaps the most widely known recent development in this area has been the "pathfinder" or "roadmap," which is intended to help an individual develop and follow a search strategy in a specific subject area.

The concerns of college and university instruction librarians in the 1980s are similar to those of school librarians. Frances Hopkins has identified these as attempting to move the content of the instruction from facts and procedures to concepts and theory, striving to gain recognition of the educational value of bibliographic instruction, and seeking recognition of instruction as a core function of librarianship.[16] To this list should be added the pursuit of effective planning strategies, from needs assessment through evaluation.

Guidance

Reading guidance, as a distinct method or function of reference service, includes identifying and locating appropriate materials and helping to interpret materials so that the reader can choose among them in terms of his or her interests and needs.[5] Many public libraries established "reader's advisory" services in the 1920s as a way of dealing with the increasing volume of queries from those that asked for advice on "best" books and the need to separate such queries from those that asked for specific information. The evolution of an administrative device into a specialized service technique was due to the public library's embracing the adult education movement from the mid-1920s onward.

The hallmarks of reading guidance are the unhurried interview, during which the reader's needs, goals, and reading habits are articulated; reading lists or reading courses, individual designed to meet the reader's needs; and friendly followup, to see that the reader gets the materials when needed and to see if changes in the list or course are needed. These core aspects of reading guidance are supported and supplemented by annotated booklists and guides that can be used to choose and to suggest appropriate materials, book talks and reviews, and a reader interest file that allows the library to notify readers of newly received books that will interest them.

In the 1940s and 1950s the public library's involvement in adult education activities moved from the era of planned reading programs and reader's advisory services into one of services to groups and finally to one of library-sponsored adult education groups. Separate reading guidance staffs began to be replaced by the provision of guidance service by the reference staff generally. While the literature of the 1950s through the 1970s has continued to discuss reader's advisory services and to distinguish between information and guidance techniques, the separate reader's advisory service has not been a prominent feature of reference service.

Recent developments in the guidance aspects of reference services have paralleled the growth of the philosophy of "special publics." This philosophy finds inadequate the concept of the "general reader" and the characterization of library users by broad occupational, educational, and socio-economic traits. Rather, librarians are recognizing that there are a very large number of distinctive user groups among the general library's clientele, each with special needs for specially adapted services. The development of effective reference services to such a special public is based on detailed study of the characteristics of the group that affect reading, learning, and information use; involvement of members of the group in planning the service and setting priorities; the development of collections of materials with particular relevance to the special group, which may involve the use of non-traditional and locally produced materials; and the use of a broad spectrum of stimulation and guidance techniques to assure that materials serve the goals of the program.[10]

Special publics to which particular attention has been given from the 1960s into the 1980s include the economically and educationally disadvantaged, the physically handicapped, the aging, persons with certain behavioral or psychological disfunctions, and persons who wish to pursue further education (especially independently and outside the classroom context). Two special guidance strategies will illustrate the adaptations that are being made to meet the needs of such special publics. These are bibliotherapy and learner's advising.

Bibliotherapy involves the use of selected reading materials to help the reader regain health or develop acceptable behavior.[19] Much of the literature on bibliotherapy is written within the context of service to persons in institutions such as hospitals or prisons. However, with the recent trend toward "mainstreaming" and returning persons with emotional and behavioral problems to their home communities, bibliotherapy outside the institution context is gaining in emphasis. In bibliotherapy the guidance process of identifying needs, selecting and interpreting materials, and encouraging their use is often performed by the librarian as a part of an interdisciplinary team of helping professionals. Librarians, psychiatrists, social workers, corrections officials, and others continue to do research and to develop principles and techniques to enhance the healthful effect of reading.

The concept of the reference librarian as "learning advisor" almost brings the guidance function full circle to its early adult education roots.[20; 21] In the past decade or so, rapidly changing technology and an ever-increasing body of knowledge, coupled with the development of various formats of independent and nontraditional education, have brought to the library needs for assistance in identifying, choosing, and pursuing independent education programs. In 1975 and 1976 nine major public libraries tested a planned learner's advisory program. This experiment and the interest it generated were part of a larger movement among libraries and other agencies to assist the many adults who choose to study and learn at their own pace in their own personal style.

The learner's adviser strategy of guidance consists of the learner and the adviser working together to develop a shared understanding of the learner's goal (for example, job advancement, academic or high school equivalency credit by examination, self-fulfillment) and the development of a learning plan. The learning plan outlines the approaches which match the goals and learning style of the learner and details the sequence of learning experiences. Implementing the learning plan frequently involves referral to other formal and informal educational agencies and organizations.

Information Services

Most libraries, whether or not they offer instructional or guidance services, provide information to users in response to identified needs. Usually, the provision of such information is made upon a request or query by the user. However, information is sometimes provided to users at the initiation of the library, in anticipation of an expressed need or in response to a need identified or even stimulated by the library. An example of this would be the selective dissemination of information programs that are common in special libraries.

The amount or type of assistance that a library will provide in response to a reference question varies from library to library and from one question to another, depending on the policy of the library, the staff available, the nature of the question, and other factors. Such assistance can range from the reference librarian's merely pointing out materials or bibliographic tools that might be of help to the user to the librarian's making an extensive search for the needed information and providing it in the form that is most appropriate to the user. The types of questions answered by library information services vary widely. A large proportion of questions asked at most reference desks are "directional" in nature; that is, they ask for information about the library, its facilities and services, etc. and can usually be answered without using reference sources or materials. Many other information needs can be served by the provision of bibliographic information. Services in this category range from the simple verification or completion of a citation to extensive bibliographic compilation and current awareness services. Questions that ask for information itself, rather than citations, can range from simple fact questions that can be answered from a single source to complex questions, whose answers require information from several sources, and requests for library-prepared reports that require synthesis of information based on critical judgment.

The process through which a reference librarian provides the answer to a reference query has a number of highly interrelated parts. One of the most important of these is the clarification of the question itself, to make sure that it represents accurately the user's information need. This aspect of reference service, referred to as the "reference interview," "question negotiation," or the "pre-search interview," involves helping the user understand and articulate the information need and making sure that the librarian understands the terms and meaning of the question.

When the reference librarian and the user have agreed upon the question in the user's terms, the librarian must analyze the question and translate it into the structure and terms of the information system and resources available to answer it. This involves such considerations as the type of information sought, the type of tool or source that is likely to provide the answer, and the index or catalog terms under which the information might be sought. Using the results of this analysis and translation or question indexing, the librarian formulates a search strategy, considering such matters as the actual sources to be consulted, the order in which they will be used, the combination of terms to be searched, and the relationships among them.

The actual search for information, especially if the user is present during the search, often involves refinement of the search strategy and further analysis of the question, as the librarian and the user learn more about the information that is available. Depending on the policies and practices of the library and the wishes of the user, the reference librarian can either perform the search for the user or provide some suggestions regarding search strategy and potential sources and let the user conduct the search.

There is also wide variation regarding the delivery of the information found by librarians in response to questions. Some libraries or the users they serve prefer that the user receive only the documents or materials containing the information, with the process of extracting and interpreting it left to the user. Other libraries, particularly special libraries, will extract information and synthesize it into a state-of-the-art report as an answer to a question that requires judgment and interpretation.

While the major features of information services were developed by the mid-twentieth century, their particular concerns and activities are continually changing, as user needs and information resources change. These changes are the subject of the conference on which this volume is based. Three examples (two of which receive more extensive coverage in later papers) will be used to illustrate these changes: cooperative reference services, computer assisted reference services, and information and referral services.

The borrowing of specific materials by one library from another on behalf of users is a long-standing practice. Codes and guidelines to regularize this library service have been developed by library associations and organizations from early in the twentieth century down to the present time. Recently, of course, the capacity of libraries to render this service has been greatly enhanced by the application of computers and telecommunication technology.

From at least as far back as the 1960s, libraries have also requested assistance from each other in the form of answers to reference questions that have not been translated into specific author-title interlibrary loan requests. The 1970s and '80s have seen a dramatic increase in such cooperative reference programs and in conferences and literature related to them.

The referring of reference questions from library to library introduces some fundamental changes into the question answering process. For example, in a cooperative reference situation the reference interview is conducted by one librarian and the search is formulated and implemented by another. The search must be conducted in the absence of the user, and the information that is found is delivered to the user without the user-searcher interaction and evaluative feedback that can enhance search effectiveness. Reference librarians and administrators are exploring and developing various means of improving the quality of cooperative reference service, especially the full exploitation of modern communications technology to maintain as much as possible the interaction between users, librarians, and information resources that characterize effective information service. For example, the format in which the reference question is transmitted from library to library (whether it be by mail, teletype, or telephone) should be designed so as to capture and transmit as much relevant and accurate information as possible about the user and the information need. At times it is appropriate to have the user in direct contact with the librarian to which the question has been referred. Policies and practices regarding such direct contact, as well as for other aspects of cooperative reference service, will continue to be developed and refined.

One of the most important developments in the information resources available to the reference librarian and the user has been the wide availability of computer searchable data bases, especially of bibliographic data, and the means for searching these data bases at any time and in an interactive mode. With technological and conceptual roots in the 1950s and before, computerized data base searching became widespread in the 1970s, and in 1981 Patricia Swanson could say that "Computerized bibliographic searches are almost commonplace in the delivery of reference services."[22]

The role of the reference librarian in assisting users with computer readable data bases is basically the same as it is with more traditional information sources. The need to clarify the question is still there, as the need for identification of and choice between potential answering sources, the translation of the question into the terms of the information source, the formulation of a search strategy, and assistance in conducting the search. On the other hand, there are also some important differences. For various reasons (including the "peep hole" effect, whereby only a small portion of the computerized information source and its structure can be seen at one time, the fact that it is costly to do a "browsing" type of search by computer, and the fact that many things must be made explicit in a computer search that can be left implicit in a traditional search), the reference process is more formal in a computer search than is typically the case in the ordinary reference query situation.

Often, the user for whom a computerized search is to be made will be given an appointment to discuss the information need and the search with a librarian (as contrasted to the "first come first served" immediate service for other users). The reference interview is usually considerably longer in this situation than for other users. The pre-search planning, including choice of potential answering sources (data bases), selection of indexing terms, and formulation of a search strategy, is done more formally and completely for a computerized search than for a traditional search. Also, it is more common for the librarian actually to conduct the search when working with a computer readable data base than is the case with manual searches in printed sources.

Just as the sheer number of information sources can be a barrier between a person who needs information and the resolution of that need, so can the number and complexity of service agencies be a barrier between a person with a problem and the agency which can help solve that problem. It has long been recognized that persons with needs for assistance (whether persons needing charity aid, persons whose lives are disrupted by war, or persons who could be served by government welfare agencies) fail to receive that assistance because they fail to find or use the agencies that exist. It has also been recognized that information and personal assistance provided by a referral service can effectively link persons who have needs or problems with agencies that can serve the needs or solve the problems. During the last decade, an increasing number of libraries, especially urban public libraries, have been including such a service, now commonly called "information and referral service" (I&R) among their reference services.[6]

While the reference process in information and referral services is basically the same as in other information services, there are some differences in particulars. The information provided is not in books or printed sources prepared by others and purchased by the library. Rather, it is found in a resource file about community agencies that has been created by the library staff. This resource file, commonly in a loose-leaf format and with detailed subject indexing, can be supplemented with vertical file pamphlets and hand-out information on the agencies.

Another important difference between information and referral service and traditional question-answering service is that I&R service does not stop with the provision of a piece of information. There is usually some sort of additional service to make sure that the link is actually made between the person and the service agency. Depending on the policies of the library and the needs of the user, this might include contacting the agency to make an appointment for the user, or even escorting the user to the agency. Most writers on I&R services emphasize the importance of followup with the user to see if the service of the agency actually helped solve his or her problem. Such followup can help the I&R service evaluate its effectiveness, can improve the accuracy of the resource file, can help keep service agencies accountable and responsive, and can lead to alternative referrals if the user was not helped by the initial one.

Summary and Conclusion

Information, instruction and guidance services in libraries have had a somewhat short period of development, beginning in the last quarter of the nineteenth century. Their broad functions of providing personal assistance to users in overcoming barriers between them and the information they need has remained the same over the years. Likewise, their essential process of identifying and clarifying the user's need, selecting information or learning resources to meet that need, and assisting the user in finding and using those resources remains unchanged. On the other hand, information, instruction, and guidance services are continually evolving, as user needs change and become better known, as information resources change and develop, and as equipment and processes for bringing users and information together are developed and refined.

The key to any personal assistance service is, of course, the staff that provides it. Reference staff members will also need to remain the same in fundamentals, such as a thorough knowledge of their users and skill in communicating with them and a thorough knowledge of information resources and skill in exploiting them on behalf of users; but they will also need continually to be changing, as users change and as the nature and structure of information resources change.

In addition to the current developments and trends already mentioned above, such as user education, computer applications, and resource sharing, the planners of the conference on which this volume is based included two other important concerns that will continue to receive major attention from reference librarians and administrators.

The first of these is the matter of direct user fees for information services. This has been brought into sharp focus by the financial problems associated with the addition of computer based searching to reference services. Access to and interactive searching of computerized data bases is quite costly, and many libraries have not been able to gain additions to their budgets to cover the costs of such service. On the other hand, it has seemed unwise to deny the service to those who would pay for it. Since computer-assisted searching is a special service, involving staff time and other service beyond that which is provided to all users and with costs that can easily be associated with specific users, administrators see some justification for direct user fees. However, many reference librarians are aware that such service is appropriate to a wide range of users, some of whom cannot pay for it, and find the inequitable access to information caused by fees contrary to their philosophy of reference service. This is a hard dilemma, exacerbated by uncertain economic conditions, which will receive much discussion, as reference librarians attempt to minimize the barriers between all their users and the information they need.

Another matter currently of major concern to information, instruction, and guidance librarians is the planning and evaluation of services. Increasingly, reference librarians are recognizing that effective services can only be based on careful identification of user needs. This involves identification of special target publics and collaboration with members of these user groups to ascertain information needs and to translate these into service goals, objectives, and priorities. Likewise, reference librarians are more and more aware of the need for accurate measurement and evaluation of their services. At the present time, most authors of the literature of reference service evaluation admit that the state of the art is fairly rudimentary, yet all agree that continued study and development will result in improvement and increased effectiveness in personal assistance to library users in pursuit of information.

NOTES

1. This paper is adapted from the author's article, "Reference," in the *ALA World Encyclopedia of Library and Information Services* (Chicago: American Library Association, 1980, pp. 864–74). Used with the permission of the publisher.

2. This section on history is based on Rothstein's study [12].

3. See reference [13]. This longer title was used for the original paper, read at the historic 1876 conference of librarians.

4. The section on instruction in library use is based on material from [14], [15], and [16].

5. The section on guidance draws heavily on [18], especially articles by Margaret E. Monroe and Helen H. Lyman.

6. The section on information and referral services is based on material from [23], [24], and [25].

REFERENCES

1. "A Commitment to Information Services: Developmental Guidelines." *RQ* 15 (Summer 1976): 327–30.

2. Rothstein, Samuel. "Reference Service: The New Dimension in Librarianship." *College and Research Libraries* 22 (January 1961): 11–18.

3. Wyer, James I. *Reference Work: A Textbook for Students of Library Work and Librarians.* Chicago: American Library Association, 1930.

4. Shera, Jesse. "Automation and the Reference Librarian." *RQ* 3 (July 1964): 3–7.

5. Rees, Alan M. "Broadening the Spectrum." In *The Present Status and Future Prospects of Reference/Information Service*, edited by Winifred B. Linderman. Chicago: American Library Association, 1967.

6. Bunge, Charles A. "Reference Service in the Information Network." In *Proceedings of the Conference on Interlibrary Communications and Information Networks*, edited by Joseph Becker. Chicago: American Library Association, 1971.

7. Jahoda, Gerald and Olson, Paul E. "Analyzing the Reference Process." *RQ* 12 (Winter 1972): 148–56.

8. Katz, William A. *Introduction to Reference Work.* 4th ed. New York: McGraw-Hill, 1982.

9. Wagers, Robert. "American Reference Theory and the Information Dogma." *Journal of Library History* 13 (Summer 1978): 265–81.

10. Monroe, Margaret E. "Emerging Patterns of Community Service." *Library Trends* 28 (Fall 1979): 129-38.

11. Kaplan, Louis. *The Growth of Reference Service in the United States from 1876 to 1893*. Chicago: Association of College and Reference Libraries, 1952 (*ACRL Monographs*, No. 2).

12. Rothstein, Samuel. *The Development of Reference Services through Academic Traditions, Public Library Practice and Special Librarianship*. Chicago: Association of College and Reference Librarians, 1955 (*ACRL Monographs*, No. 14).

13. Green, Samuel S. "Personal Relations between Librarians and Readers." *American Library Journal* 1 (October 1876): 74-81.

14. Farber, Evan I. and Kirk, Thomas G., Jr. "Instruction in Library Use." In *The ALA Yearbook, 1976*. Chicago: American Library Association, 1976.

15. Lubans, John, Jr. *Educating the Library User*. New York: Bowker, 1974.

16. Hopkins, Frances L. "A Century of Bibliographic Instruction: The Historical Claim to Professional and Academic Legitimacy." *College and Research Libraries* 43 (May 1982): 192-98.

17. "Guidelines for Bibliographic Instruction in Academic Libraries." *College and Research Libraries News* 4 (April 1977): 92.

18. Monroe, Margaret E., ed. *Reading Guidance and Bibliotherapy in Public, Hospital and Institutional Libraries: A Selection of Papers*. Madison: Library School of the University of Wisconsin, 1971.

19. Rubin, Rhea J. "Use of Bibliotherapy in Response to the 1970s." *Library Trends* 28 (Fall 1979): 239-52.

20. Toro, Jose O. "Independent Study in Public Libraries." In *The ALA Yearbook, 1976*. Chicago: American Library Association, 1976.

21. Boles, Suzanne and Smith, Barbara D. "The Learner's Advisory Service." *Library Trends* 28 (Fall 1979): 165-78.

22. Swanson, Patricia K. "Reference Services." In *The ALA Yearbook, 1981*. Chicago: American Library Association, 1981.

23. Croneberger, Robert, Jr. and Luck, Carolyn. "Defining Information and Referral Service." *Library Journal* 100 (November 1, 1975): 1984–87.

24. Croneberger, Robert, Jr. and Luck, Carolyn. "I&R = Reference." *Library Journal* 101 (January 15, 1976): 318–19.

25. Anthony, Carolyn. "Information and Referral Service." In *The ALA Yearbook, 1981*. Chicago: American Library Association, 1981.

The Role of Reference Service in the Mission of the Academic Library

Herbert White

While I accept this topic as somewhat tongue in cheek, and assume that there is no one who would argue that academic libraries should not perform reference service, the level of that service as provided in academic libraries, and particularly large academic libraries, varies substantially from that in public libraries, and especially in special libraries. These librarians in particular would argue that the only point in having a collection at all is for the use which is made of it, and that material which is not used is therefore wasted. Operations research people would probably agree with this, since they would postulate that it is harder to find things in a large collection than in a smaller one, and that material which is not used therefore inhibits the location of material which is used. They would argue that we should weed continuously and ruthlessly, even if we have plenty of space.

While these are not necessarily generally held sentiments, I do recall the statement, made not by an academic librarian but by a library school dean, that our job is to provide the material in the collection. Whether or not it is used is not our problem. We also have the rather famous quote attributed to one of our revered academic library leaders (and a quote which I first considered a joke until assured of its accuracy) that "we will be remembered not for the service we gave but for the collection we left behind us." Exaggerated as some of these expressions may be, they are nevertheless based on some level of acceptance. There are clear indications that the academic library, unlike certainly the special library, does not consider active or even aggressive service from the collection as a primary goal, or even as goal at all. It is argued that the academic library is primarily geared to be a self-service library, that for students this is desirable or expected, and that faculty insist on doing their own work. Therefore, even when we perform reference services for students the main intent is to avoid having to do it in the future. We teach them so that they can serve themselves. Much of the emphasis on bibliographic instruction is to develop library users who can function on their own.

Special librarians, whose own contribution to the objectives of the organization may be measured more tangibly, but whose users come to them largely from the academic community, complain that these users are passive, accept low levels of service without complaint, and have no expectations of professional interaction. Their only expectation is for the development of a collection, and that really translates more directly into the desire that the library purchase materials not for the library but for immediate transfer to their own offices. It is a concept of library service which I, perhaps simplistically and uncharitably, have termed the free bookstore as one of the fringe benefits to offset low salaries.

It can be argued, and frequently is, that whether or not this emphasis on collection instead of on service from the collection is the best approach, it is the approach on which the academic community insists. However, that argument can be probed, and under intense scrutiny it begins to show cracks.

It has been my observation that the individuals in the library accorded the highest level of professional recognition and regard by faculty are not the specialists who acquire and process, but those who actually work with the material's content. These individuals are the subject specialists or bibliographers, and the branch librarians who frequently work as special librarians, doing what Grieg Aspnes would describe as taking the burden of the work off the user's shoulders. Just leave me the problem, and I will get back to you. Aspnes would state that this is in fact what most library users (including faculty) would really prefer if they thought it were acceptable to ask for it — that for most faculty members there is no particular thrill in digging in the library and the task is frequently shunted to graduate students. Aspnes and other special librarians would argue that their clients, who are frequently academic degree holders at various levels including the Ph.D. only one stage removed from the academic library experience, come to the special library expecting nothing except the ordering of material on request, and must be weaned to a higher level of expectations. They would further state that once they recognize that librarians can and will do reference work, that they can probably do it better, and that it is not immoral or unethical to have this work done for them, they become addicted. Some of them continue to demand reference service well beyond retirement.

There is growing evidence that the so-called Madame Curie model of research, of trying to learn everything on a subject and then sorting it out to determine where the truth lies, is not the way most research is conducted. Most library work is not in support of the search for knowledge, it is in support of evidence to further conclusions (or if you prefer paradigms) already reached. This kind of applied research actually resembles much of what happens in special libraries, and a considerable amount of it is because of the influence of government grants and contracts. Osburn has argued that this change has even affected humanities researchers, who do not really want to be pointed at stack ranges of raw materials but the specific page or chapter or article or book which proves the point. Osburn[1] argues, and I would concur, that academic library operational philosophies are not geared to this kind of library use at all, except perhaps in some branch libraries.

The wide-spread premise that we do not help students very much because faculty do not want them helped is not really borne out by observation and experience, either. If this were true, then faculty would to a far greater extent assure that the materials necessary for the self-education process were available, and they would coordinate far more closely with the library to map out a program of student library education for the course in question. In truth, faculty frequently make assignments without bothering to determine whether or not the material is available. Like the law professor played by John Houseman in "Paper Chase," they may even consider it a part of the learning experience to cast the student adrift to shift for himself or herself, and any way to obtain the answer is acceptable as long as it is obtained. Most would not condone outright plagiarism, but there is certainly enough known and acknowledged activity in co-operation, the use of test files, term paper models, coaching sessions for athletes and others, and a variety of other tactics, to convince at least me that for most academicians the accomplishment outweighs the concern about how that accomplishment was reached.

As a final point, and perhaps the most delicately sensitive one, I would argue that it is simply not true that faculty members are experts who fully know their own literature. There is really no way that they could, given its growth both in size and interdisciplinary characteristics. At the same time, faculty can hardly admit to themselves let alone others that they do not keep up, or that there are things they should know which they do not know. And so *their* ignorance is the most dangerous of all, an ignorance which masquerades as knowledge. We cannot really blame them for this, because they see no choice. An admission of a knowledge gap is not acceptable if there is no indication that the gap can be closed. It only leads to an admission of permanent incompetence. I have had Ph.D. scientists who are doing industrial research but who have poor library service tell me quite straightforwardly that the five journals they read contain everything they need to keep abreast of in their field. How could they say anything else?

This narrow focus on the function of academic libraries, as

orderers, arrangers and distributors of requested material, causes particular problems in the 1980s and probably will in the foreseeable future. These problems certainly began to emerge in the mid and latter 1970s. Up to then, the historical emphasis on the library as a self-service collection to be made as complete as possible had served at least some of us reasonably well. There was money for collections, there was money for new library buildings. Innovative and entrepreneurial administrators could not only keep pace with the literature growth, but they could score some coups through the acquisition of a special collection or the development of a national or international unique strength. Satisfaction could be gained from statistics of growth, and from new impressive buildings and offices. Despite this general feeling of euphoria, in which library administrators did what they wanted to do because these were the very values which attracted them to the field, in which faculty were calm if not totally content (are they ever?), and in which academic administrators bragged about the value of the library as much as about the record of the football team, we paid a price, too. That price came because what we did in acquiring, tagging, and processing (what Fairthorne[2] calls marking and parking) was not clearly understood, particularly in terms of its intellectual component and therefore faculty equivalence. Librarians may have faculty status, but except for a very few, perhaps not even the director, acceptance into full faculty collegiality is not generally extended. This may be partly our own fault, because the mysteries of the bibliographic and analytical rites which result in occult marking on cards have never been understood, nor has their relevance been made clear. This is particularly true when faculty read in the *Chronicle of Higher Education*, their professional journal, or even the local newspaper that the Library of Congress makes all bibliographic information available to all libraries, and that anything can be identified and obtained from anywhere via satellite. However, recent history only provides a sharper focus for what has really plagued us all along. I recall repeated battles in special library settings with personnel administrators and wage and salary analysts, who could easily understand why reference and bibliographic work required professional education and training, but who could not comprehend why cataloging or the adaptation of other cataloging could not be done by a clerk or a para-professional. And, of course, judging by staffing changes in academic libraries in the 1970s they may have been prophetically correct.

As a sidelight, it is startling and perhaps refreshing to hear of some of the changes in emphasis. In a retreat sponsored by the Council on Library Resources which I attended in June 1982, I heard Robert Vosper, certainly one of our most distinguished leaders in research librarianship, stress that the greatest need in academic library administrators was now for individuals strong in areas of business management, conversant with publishing and legal ramifications, understanding of national and international systems and technological implications, and sensitive to people and issues of personnel administration. If Vosper is correct, it is not surprising that there has been so much turnover in academic library directorships.

However, there are other and perhaps more pressing needs to change, and for embracing reference activities at the highest level — what I like to call information intermediation. These needs come primarily from an impossibility to meet present faculty expectations of what a library should be. I addressed some of these in my article "Between Scylla and Charybdis" in the *Journal of Academic Librarianship,*[3] and will not repeat them here. My main reason for stating that we need to change the direction of academic libraries from a passive to an active role, convincing or over-riding the conservative faculty, comes from a less scholarly source — my old tennis coach, who said "Always change a losing game. Try something." Providing more interactive information services, or just providing some interactive information services, may be the something to try. We may not yet be facing match point, but we have probably lost at least a set by now. There are several factors which must be incorporated into the need to change. All of these have really been noted before, by a variety of writers and speakers.

It will be impossible in the future if indeed it ever was possible to keep up with materials demand as the primary emphasis. The growth in the literature, estimated at between 2 percent and 8 percent per year (and it should be noted that journal publishing unlike monographic publishing is fairly impervious to the economic crunch because of the peculiarities of cash flow), must be multiplied by price increases of publishing, which are accelerated both by the rapid growth in labor, paper and postage costs, and by the virtual disappearance of individual subscribers to scholarly journals to help defray the cost. We are the victims or beneficiaries of fluctuations in international monetary exchange rates without being able to control or predict them. Despite overall reductions in academia, new programs get started, and old ones hardly ever die. Maintaining collection equivalence would probably require an annual material budget increase of about 15 percent. That is a doubling every five years. It is not going to happen. We must shift the emphasis away from collection as the sole or primary value of the library because we are not going to be able to keep pace.

There are also substantial changes taking place in the structure of the literature with which we deal. I have already mentioned that it becomes more complex as it becomes more interdisciplinary. There are also substantial changes in access to information. The most obvious one is the growth of machine readable data bases, at first in the physical sciences, then in the social sciences, now in the humanities, soon everywhere. There is no consistency in the structure of data bases and in the search strategies needed to access them. To some extent, there probably will never be nor should there necessarily be, unless we are prepared to trade sophistication for ease of searching. The programs which attempt to provide a unified search approach to a variety of data bases invariably must reduce these systems to a common denominator, and common denominators are usually small numbers. Data base searching is a skill which can be developed at a variety of levels, and it is important that we understand the differences. I can drive a car, but I am not ready to drive at LeMans, Daytona, or Indianapolis. It is important that we understand, and that users understand, that even a knowledge of the literature (and I have some doubts about that) does not automatically bring with it a knowledge of how to access that literature. We have consistently railed against the failure of university graduates to be able to use the indexing tools of their own disciplines. In large part this is because nobody taught them how, and this is because their own professors did not think it important enough. We have always assumed that academics wanted to search their own literature, despite evidence indicating that for most of them it is not true. Project INTREX as designed by MIT, MEDLARS as developed by the National Library of Medicine, the NASA Information Facility which I headed and which developed what is now the DIALOG search system, all were based on the premise that researchers were just dying to get at those terminals. With rare and specialized exceptions, it just is not true. Searching is keying, and keying is a clerical task. They will delegate it if they can, particularly if they do not know how and do not want to admit they do not know. But we have to let them know it is all right to delegate this task, and not outside the permissible for their professional field. At least, that is the special library experience. Freer bibliographic access virtually to anyone's file through any terminal, and rapid document delivery systems for a fee — and who can doubt that they will get more rapid, cheaper, and better quality as we improve the technology of satellite and telephone communication, have lost us our monopoly for bibliographic access. Up until now, until we got through cataloging it and put it into the file, presumably nobody was allowed to know it even existed. That is a distinction we have now lost, but it is a distinction which really was not worth having in the first place.

We can and must establish a new level of expertise of our own, one which concentrates on the literature of a discipline. The argument essentially states that you may be a renowned anthropologist but you are not necessarily expert in the rapidly changing literature of your field, or certainly of allied fields. This is our expertise, and working together we can achieve maximum results. Telling the faculty all this may have some value, but many will not believe us. Their idea of what librarians are and do is too ingrained. It is better to show them, and this is why any library policy which tends to thwart the already low level of demand for reference work, particularly in the use of computer aided systems, is unthinkable because it is so self-defeating. Of course there are problems. The most significant of these, which I attempted to identify in a column in *American Libraries*,[4] revolves around the nature and inflexibility of line item budgets in general, and library budgets in particular. The historic nature of most academic library budgets, as we identified them through our studies for the National Science Foundation, effectively precommits the entire budget and leaves nothing to initiative of entrepreneural decision making. Between 60 percent and 70 percent of the budget is committed to ongoing staff salaries, and there are few options here except through resignation and retirement, and these fall not where we plan them but where happenstance places them. Most of the rest of the funds, perhaps between 20 percent and 30 percent, are allocated to the purchase of materials, and few options exist here as well. Periodical expenditures, except where cancellations are forced down unwilling throats, are pre-committed, and so to an increasing extent are book expenditures when we recognize that the political process requires that "key" or "senior" faculty members be heeded at least part of the time, and that many libraries in fact allocate their materials budgets by funds or departments. This is not necessarily bad, but it trades the perception of equity (or perhaps even the reality of equity) against the loss of maneuverability. Collection development officers have told me that as budgets get tight decisions actually get fewer, because little remains after we have bought what must be bought. I had not thought about it that way, and that is certainly not the way we teach collection building, but I am sure it is true.

We have neither enough money for people nor enough money for material. That is a harsh truth, but it has always been true, even in the more affluent 1960s. Our appetites, or perhaps I should say faculty appetites, have always exceeded capability. Given the reality of academic funding, the chances of securing additional funds for personnel staffing to do what we currently do is nil. Problems of backlogs and even of lack of support personnel have no real significance to academic administrators, who really have no plans or expectations for the library except the hope that it will stay within the allocated budget and that the faculty and the students, in that order, will not complain too strenuously about it. When you argue that you need more people because circulation has grown or because backlogs have doubled those arguments are meaningless. Only the size of the collection, as related to that of other institutions or other academic programs, has significance, because deterioration at that point can be seen as directly threatening the individual's own peer evaluation. It is for these reasons that money to supplement the library materials budget can sometimes be cadged from reluctant administrators, either in the form of special allocation or through year-end funds. Personnel funds, on the other hand, are never supplemented, and neither is the catch-all category called "all other," which, in more or less 10 percent of the budget, covers such a multitude of programs as photocopy, postage, travel, telephone, and supplies. If there are library expenditures in such areas as interlibrary borrowing or on-line search changes, they must be funded from this already impoverished category, and Parkinson as well as practical experience tell us that it is this "all other" category which, in any organization, be it the private, academic, or government sector, is in the worst shape. We not only do not have any money with which to do *new* things, we do not have any money to do *any*thing in these budget categories.

Libraries have had some success in reducing technical processing labor costs, but they have not reallocated these resources. For the most part the savings have gone to pay salary increases to retain present positions, to upgrade the inadequate dollars provided in the original budget, and in a few cases as transfers to the materials budget.

We therefore must face the unpleasant truth that we will not get more money, and undoubtedly not enough money, for present level operations except perhaps, and only perhaps, for materials. University administrators have no objectives for academic libraries except to avoid trouble. In one library with which I am well familiar the suggestion that additional funds be allocated to provide for an online circulation system was met with the answer that the faculty should be consulted as to whether they would rather have this or additional funds for the materials budget. If that sort of question is appropriate, then so is the question would you rather have money for the library materials budget or as highly paid a university president, and the answer is probably just as predictable.

Despite this depressing observation, there are some basic management truths we must bear in mind, and in my experience they are just as valid in academia as in industry and government. There are two of these truths I would share with you today. One — in the absence of money there is always some money around, and two — it is usually easier to get a lot of money than a little bit of money. Money is provided for those things which people really need or at least say they really need. The proven tactic of confrontation and assertive management is to offer a service, make it wanted, and then make sure the blame is properly allocated if that service is curtailed. The risk of confrontation and assertive management is that you can get fired. But there are worse things, and in some academic situations, they cannot even fire you — just shuffle you around.

Faculty pressures are the most effective in producing results, but even student concern can help. In one Big Ten university a new undergraduate library, actually nothing more than an undergraduate reading room, became the campus number one priority when the problem was broached by student groups to the state legislature. At another university, this one in the southeast, additional funds to expand undergraduate library services were somehow found when students began dropping in at the president's home on campus to inquire politely if they could study at his house because the library was so crowded and noisy.

And so I would argue that libraries need to switch resources as rapidly as possible and as these resources can be freed to highly visible public services, particularly intellectual services, and most particularly services to faculty and administration. Reference services provide, in my judgment, the one great potential opening for the academic library — because there is so little of it done at present, at least as compared to other types of libraries, and because needs for it are almost open-ended. Once people become addicted to it they cannot get enough. This should not surprise us. We are a service oriented society. We have not only a profusion of automotive services to fix our cars and to advise us specifically about our mufflers and our transmissions. We also have tax return services which prepare Forms 1040A, which practically anyone can do themselves in about 10 minutes. We have analysts at sport telecasts who explain to us what we just saw, and analysts after presidential speeches who tell us what we just heard. The rapid growth of the information service sector is a clear indication that people are willing to spend money for information services. This would be expected naturally enough in industry, but we also find academicians buying information services, sometimes from grant and contract funds, sometimes with organizational overhead funds. We already know that even if we charge for online search services and interlibrary loan services some individuals will pay. However, I think that such charges, although perhaps politically attractive, are the wrong direction in which to head, in part because it develops even on the campus an elite of information rich and of information poor (frequently humanists), but perhaps even more importantly because it would lower our collegial esteem. Academicians deal with those who deal with money because they must, but they do not consider it a proper academic activity.

Even if I were to have convinced you up to now, you would still face the additional problem of how your budget is put together by the budget administration and accounting people with whom you deal. It is a line item budget, and it allocates dollars not in terms of the services they provide but in the way the checks are written. What little money there is for reference services is in the people budget. Therefore, assuming you already have reference librarians bought and paid for they can happily run through the stacks answering reference questions, as long as they use material already there, because that category has already been expensed. It would be preferable if, in doing research work, they not have to use the long distance telephone, because although that use might save hours of work, the telephone call is not paid for and the hours of work are. Similarly, online search costs are incremental charges, and they are not budgeted. This then makes them expensive, even in those instances in which it can be proven that a machine search is in fact cheaper to perform. It does not matter, because the one search is already prepaid and the other is not.

It is yet another indication of the passivity (or perhaps indifference) of the library user that they accept our explanation of having to pass along to them the cost of machine searches, or even the cost of interlibrary loan, because our budgets are not designed to absorb them. Sometimes we do this under the premise that these are "non-traditional" services, when in fact they are simply variants in the information supply business and the only thing which is non-traditional is the budget approach.

You may be glad that you do not have me in your academic community when I tell you that I refuse to accept pass-along charges in either the area of interlibrary loan or of online searching. I suspect that I have gotten away with this in part because I use neither of these services very extensively, because as a dean I do pose something of a threat, or perhaps because I am considered something of an eccentric who has to be humored as long as the cost is not prohibitive. However, I consider the issues anything but trivial, and it is my contention that by refusing to accept these transfer costs I am according the library the professional respect as expert in its own field which it deserves, and then also making it bear the responsibility for its professional decisions. My arguments run along relatively simple lines.

Interlibrary borrowing is an alternative to purchase, and certainly a reasonable one. No library can afford to buy everything, but the determination of what it purchases and what it does not and therefore has to borrow is one which the library staff is supposed to make. I obviously would prefer, ideally, that the library anticipated all my needs and purchased everything I plan to request in the future. Failing that, I refuse to be doubly penalized, first by the time delay in their failure to have the material, and secondly because they plan to make me pay the charges which their decision has incurred. Interlibrary borrowing is a materials cost and should be budgeted accordingly. Doing this would provide some easy cross-over points between repeated borrowing and purchase, and almost automatically wipe out violations of the copyright law because items borrowed that frequently, if the same budget had to pay for them, would become quickly unattractive as candidates for borrowing and would probably be purchased.

With regard to online searching, my response to the question "would you like to have an online search" (although I am no longer asked that question) is "why are you asking me? You are the reference librarian, use whatever approaches you consider most appropriate in your professional judgment." A number of libraries, both special and academic, have established their machine search operations as separate from their reference departments, to separate the accounting costs. I think it is a big mistake, because it establishes online searching as some sort of hot house exotic plant rarely found in libraries. It is not difficult to predict that in the very near future online searching will be the bread and butter of library reference, because in many cases it will be more complete, faster, and cheaper. All we have to figure out is how to budget it. That is not an easy task, but it is the most fundamental issue we have to solve if we are going to do anything even remotely innovative. The present line item expenditures which identify labor costs by individual salary, and materials costs not only by type of material (book, serial, microform) but also by subject discipline, leave us no options and no flexibility. What we need is program budgeting, and the program category we need to establish is something called information access, instead of materials purchase. Information access consists of a variety of things — most obviously the purchase of material, but also interlibrary borrowing and online access charges to data bases which contain reference tools we did not buy. SUNY Albany has been able to do something like this in its budgeting process, but there are not many others of whom I am aware.

It obviously is not easy. It requires wresting control over the library decision processes away from the faculty, and centralizing it in the library. It is not easy to do because campus administrators have no interest in antagonizing the faculty on our behalf and because faculty have no expectations beyond the emphasis on size as a measure of quality and no real appreciation of the librarian's role in the intellectual processes of academia. When the president of the United States, the Secretary of the Department of Education, and university presidents appoint non-librarians to key library posts it is a clear indication of that lack of perception. They would not do this for appointments in the legal or medical fields. And yet, at the same time, we see examples of librarians who are accorded respect and status by their faculty colleagues. Invariably, it is not the keepers and processors of the warehouse. It is those individuals who work with them, and who assist them directly, in work with content and analysis, in problem solving. My conclusion then is obviously that indeed academic librarians need to do reference work, and a lot more reference work than they currently do. How much? For starters, we could look at the special library model, which has transferred many of the acquisitions and processing costs to clerks and paraprofessionals, and which now expends at least twice the professional effort on user services as on technical services. Academic libraries have also reduced the professional level of technical services, but those saved funds have not been identified and transferred, and they have been gobbled up in the daily struggle to survive. Even in public services, we run the risk of falling into a trap. The most visible activity in libraries is clerical routine, and the danger is that in the absence of adequate budgets clerical services will drive out professional services, unless we establish value systems and priorities which prevent this from happening. I could argue with some assurance that for academic libraries the ratio of professional service activities should be even greater, because of the complexity, bulk, and interdisciplinary nature of the resources, and because there are fewer tools, particularly in the humanities. I would suggest that at least some, although certainly not all, of our academic scholars slog through the research process not because they want to but because they have to. They have no one to whom to delegate it, and they consider it imprudent to even think about whether they would like to be able to delegate it. One of my most interesting conversion projects in industrial consulting activities is to remind researchers in such organizations as chemical companies that they are not being paid to undertake research, they are being paid to produce research results. There is nothing immoral in delegation, if this process is effective and if you can find someone competent to whom to delegate. That competence, I also remind them, extends beyond an understanding of the subject field. It includes an understanding of the literature of that field, the literature of allied fields, and a comprehension of the skills necessary to access that literature through increasingly complex data bases and search protocols. By that time, usually except for German chemists, they are prepared to concede not only that there are some things which librarians could do as well, but even that there are some things librarians could do better.

That is the industrial model, but does it differ so greatly from the academic model? Not according to researchers such as Ladd and Lipseth, who report their findings in the *Chronicle of Higher Education*. According to them, even in major universities the faculty undertaking broad exploratory research is less than 10 percent of the total. The rest are either looking for proofs or solutions (just as their industrial brothers and sisters are) or are really doing no research at all.

And so we need to do much more reference work — and by reference work I have already stated that whether we approach it through a data base, a published handbook, the card catalog, or a directory is an internal decision we do not even need to broach with the client. We need to do it because the public needs it. We also need to do it because we need it. An emphasis on collection rather than on service is for the present and the foreseeable future a no-win game, bound to lose us status and friends. It will ultimately get us bypassed by other services. Needs stimulate services, and not just in the for-profit sector. A class project by one of my colleagues at Indiana University to identify the number of information centers on campus unearthed well over forty, and that certainly was not a complete list. Most of them did not know of the existence of others in overlapping areas, and many were unknown to the library. They sprang up because there was a need, a need which was not being filled. What these information centers do is in most cases relatively simple. It includes screening the larger mass of literature for items of more specific interest, usually on fairly broad topical areas such as diabetes or railway transportation. When done by computer we now call this SDI, but alert and aggressive librarians were doing it long before then, if only by flagging specific items for the attention of readers. Some of these information centers publish newsletters and bulletins, most do reference work, many compile bibliographies. They do this for the same academic faculty members we presumably serve, in part because they want it done, and in part because nobody else, certainly not the academic library, has stepped forward to do it. And there is money available for these operations, some externally and some internally supplied. There is usually money for what is wanted badly enough.

Let me leave you with a few simple if perhaps startling statistics. Lee Burchinal,[5] former head of the National Science Foundation Office of Science Information Services, has estimated that the number of online searches grew from a start in 1968 to about one million per year in 1975, with a quadrupling to 4,000,000 by 1980. If he is correct, we may be well beyond 5,000,000 as I write. If you think that is a lot of searches, please recognize that even if all the searches had been performed for scientists and engineers, which they obviously were not, it still only adds up to one search per technical professional every six months. The future growth of online searching is virtually beyond our ability to estimate. There can be little doubt that it will represent much of the substance, if not the backbone, of the use of library materials. If we choose not to be involved, because we are too busy doing other things, or because the cost distribution formulas do not meet our preconceptions of what budgets should look like, these searches will most assuredly be done. They will be done by others, as in many locations they already are. However, from there it is but a short step to the decision that while we indeed want physical collections of books and journals, we may not need librarians to manage them.

NOTES

1. Osburn, Charles B. *Academic Research and Library Resources: Changing Patterns in America.* Greenwood Press, Westport, CT, 1979.

2. Fairthorne, Robert A. *Towards Information Retrieval.* Butterworths, London, 1961.

3. White, Herbert S. "Library Materials Prices and Academic Library Practices: Between Scylla and Charybdis." *Journal of Academic Librarianship* 5:20–23, March 1979.

4. White, Herbert S. "Who Pays for 'Peripheral' Services, and What Are They Anyway?" *American Libraries* 13:40, 44, January 1982.

5. Burchinal, Lee G. "The S&T Communication Enterprise in the United States. Status and Forecasts." *Library Science with a Slant to Documents (India)* 14: 53–61, June 1977.

Reference and the Other Technical Services
in a Large University Library

William Miller

We rarely define reference service as having much relationship to technical services, though even a moment's reflection would make it obvious that there must be important connections between them. Most definitions of reference derive from the obvious activities usually conducted on a day-to-day basis within reference departments. Bill Katz's common sense notion that reference "may be defined as answering questions,"[1] or Donald Davinson's circular description of reference as "the activity undertaken by librarians and associated types of staff from reference libraries"[2] are typical expressions of how most of us perceive reference. We all have an operational sense of what reference service is, or at least what it has been, in the same way that we all have a notion of what a chair is, though it might be difficult for any of us to frame a definition that includes all chairs. My operational definition includes such things as answering questions at the reference desk, over the phone, and through the mail; doing library instruction of various kinds; creating bibliographic aids of various lengths and levels of complexity; conducting database searches; indexing local publications to facilitate access; and maintaining vertical or clipping files of various kinds. Interlibrary loan and government documents work are also closely connected in most people's minds with reference work, and the rationale for such an association leads me to my own usual definition of reference work: library work which includes continual interaction with the library's external users, and which requires a substantive knowledge of the library's information resources.

That is a rather broad definition, and you can probably poke some holes in it, since, for example, it very well may include circulation and information desk activities. This does not particularly bother me, though it might bother some reference librarians to admit that such areas do, whether or not we like it, serve reference functions if only in a broad sense. This definition does have the merit of allowing me to define technical services as including cataloging, collection development, binding, and any other function which, however highly skilled it may be, does not include routine contact with the public.

Such is my operating definition of reference, and it serves well enough on a daily basis. Yet it has been increasingly apparent that something has been missing in my equation. That something is the role of technical services in reference work. What started me thinking about this role was an article in a recent issue of the *RTSD Newletter* concerning online catalogs. The University of Illinois is developing an online catalog based on WLN (Washington Library Network) software, and the fuller WLN records are going to be bumping off the shorter records currently in the LCS (Library Control System) circulation system when records match. About one-fifth of the resulting database will contain the fuller WLN records, and the remaining four-fifths will continue to be the old LCS short records. What bothered me was this statement: "It is assumed that the mix of LCS records and full records for newer material will generally satisfy user needs."[3] That statement may very well be true, but I do not think that any reference librarian would ever make it. We think much more about the needs of researchers, and simply do not think in terms of providing percentages of satisfaction for some users to the detriment of other users. When I was doing my Ph.D. dissertation, it was not enough to know that the library had an 1888 edition of a work; I needed to know *which* 1888 edition. While most users may not care about the fullness of cataloging records, scholars will most likely need to know the information in the full records, and be handicapped by the lack of it.

As Thomas, Hinckley, and Eisenbach say, "the future of the catalog is too important to be entrusted only to technical services librarians and administrators."[4] I do not say this to denigrate technical services people, but merely to suggest that they, too, are doing reference work, though they may be doing it in a vacuum or at one remove from the public. Technical services people create the tools with which people find their information, and the atmosphere in which they find it. It is quite artificial, therefore, to divorce reference from the other services in the library and discuss it as though it were an extricable part of the totality of what libraries do. Therefore, I should like to pay some attention to the connections between reference and technical services, to suggest that "reference librarians have responsibilities in helping to determine how the library can best make the necessary, difficult adjustments" caused by automation of technical services,[5] and to discuss the degree to which reference itself might be considered as one of the technical services, or requires a mastery of them.

It is mostly in the large university libraries that the line between public and technical services is now blurring. Most people might guess that the small college library environment provides much more opportunity for interaction between the two areas, and it is true that in smaller libraries it is much more likely that technical services people have to staff reference desks during evenings and weekends if the library is to be able to staff the desk at all. The small college reference librarian is also more likely to be involved in collection development for the general library collection than is the reference librarian in a university. On the whole, however, the traditional functions remain largely static in college libraries today. This may change as companies develop economical turnkey systems appropriate for small libraries, but on the whole there has not been the money or the impetus available to break down traditional barriers. Manual systems are generally efficient and manageable in small libraries, and demands for service do not strain resources unduly. Therefore, in most cases it is possible to continue to do things as they have always been done.

In most university libraries, on the other hand, most manual systems have either disappeared or are faced with extinction in the near future because of the expense, time, and labor needed to maintain them. Reference librarians have done fairly well in adapting themselves to the new technologies which their libraries have been able to afford to purchase. Most ARL reference departments, for instance, now make regular use of OCLC (Online Computer Library Center), RLIN (Research Libraries Information Network), and other such databases in their work, and a recent survey by Baker and Kluegel indicates that about half of all large reference departments have OCLC terminals, though not all these are yet made directly available to the public.[6]

Of course the most successful example of a breakdown in the artificial barriers between public and technical services has occurred in the area of circulation, which is today the most highly integrated area of librarianship. Reference librarians have been less successful at incorporating these "circulation" databases into their work than they have been with the incorporation of the "cataloging" databases, and there are still too many university reference desks which have no public-access circulation terminals. Many reference librarians have not perceived the relevance of circulation records to their work; for instance, even without searchable subject headings in the circulation file, the ability to browse in sequence by call number, author's name, or first word of a title can provide important and quick subject access to the collection. Of course circulation records *are* now incorporating searchable subject headings as part of the records of major bibliographic utilities now being used to expand the circulation files. As circulation files gradually assume additional functions such as assigned reading and in-process functions, and as they become replacements for manual reference card catalogs, the failure to recognize their value will undoubtedly be rectified. Reference librarians will be forced, willy-nilly, to use them.

In university libraries today you will find reference librarians sitting as members of automation committees and helping to make library-wide decisions about technical service matters with wide implications for public service. You will also find a few reference librarians with a thorough knowledge of technical service matters; these will mostly be people who have formerly worked in technical services, or who currently have some sort of dual appointment in which, for instance, they catalog science materials half-time and work at a science reference desk the rest of the time. On the whole, however, there is a general lack of hard knowledge about technical service activities among reference librarians — a lack of knowledge about the many clerical routines, and also a lack of knowledge about the rules which govern the catalogs. It is probably also true that technical service librarians lack a knowledge of basic reference tools, and a knowledge of the way in which questions must be negotiated, among other things. Yet most catalogers could come out to spend half of their time at the reference desk and give tolerably good service after a relatively short period of training. Most reference librarians, on the other hand, would need extensive training of a kind beyond practicality in order to spend half time as catalogers while maintaining their reference responsibilities.

Why this disparity in versatility exists has always fascinated me. Why should it be so? Friends of mine who are catalogers tell me that they are more capable of dealing with detail than we reference librarians are, and that cataloging is a more rigorous discipline than reference librarianship. I am not much impressed with this belief; for one thing, reference librarians search the various on-line databasis such as ERIC (Educational Resources Information Center) or Medline with as great an exactitude as catalogers do their work. Nor do I believe in the old tale of catalogers having vastly different personalities. There may be minor aggregate differences, and some people clearly gravitate to one area or another. But surely the similarities between reference librarians and catalogers must be much more significant than the differences. To a great extent the question of whether one becomes a reference librarian or a cataloger, or anything else, depends on the nature of the job market, and on the first job which one obtains. If that first job is a reference position, it is unlikely that the individual will ever become a cataloger.

The reason for the disparity between the reference librarians' versatility and that of their cataloging colleagues lies rather in the difference in the nature of the work itself. Consider, first of all, the work in the reference department of an ARL library which serves a large undergraduate population in addition to a large number of graduate students, faculty, and assorted members of the public.[7] When the reference librarians in this department are not doing database searches, class lectures, handouts, indexing, weeding, ordering of new reference books, or a variety of other tasks, they are working on the reference desk for approximately fifty percent of the time. They may serve only two-hour shifts during the week when many people are available; they will spend four or eight hours on the desk during evenings and weekends. During the hours that they are on the desk, the pace of business will, of course, vary. On the whole, however, business will be quite brisk, and it will not be unusual for one hundred inquiries to come to the desk during a single hour, both in person and over the telephone. Even if the department is fortunate enough to be able to staff with three librarians on the desk at one time, reference librarians have only a minute of two, on the average, to handle each inquiry which comes their way.

The effect of this pressure is not widely understood or appreciated outside of reference departments.[8] As the only reference librarian at a small college library, I was on duty eight hours every day, but never felt fatigued by it, and in fact had considerable amounts of time during the day to do a variety of chores, many of which required much concentration. I could not have imagined how much more complex and pressure-filled the university reference experience is. I can only compare it to working as a cook at McDonald's during the lunch-time rush, except that along with the barrage of requests for cheeseburgers and fish sandwiches, people are also regularly asking for coq au vin, cheese souffle, and chocolate mousse — and expecting you to prepare it all, and fast. It may well be true, as so many are so fond of asserting, that eighty percent of reference questions are directional or mundane in some way. But the sheer volume of these questions, coupled with the steady interspersing of difficult and complex questions, makes university library reference work a frenetic enterprise, and the constant shifting of mental gears causes a fatigue beyond all proportion to what the individual questions might cause if asked in isolation. I have occasionally had the experience of redoing in tranquility a reference question originally encountered during the heat of battle, and the difference in my ability to handle the question is truly astounding.

The work of the cataloger, on the other hand, I would compare to that of the chef at a French restaurant. The restaurant can only seat so many people at a time, and, while the chef is busy, he is not frantically busy; indeed, no one wants him to be frantically busy, because he might ruin the meal which would be unacceptable to the management. So the tasks, though varied and extensive, are known, the amount of work is limited, and the patrons make appointments for service. He has to prepare the coq au vin, the souffle, and the mousse — but he does such work continually, and has been training for it for years. Rarely is he ever asked to prepare a dish he has never encountered before; indeed, he works from a menu containing a finite number of well-known dishes with which he has much experience.

Like all analogies, this one is not perfect. For one thing, the cataloging of a book presents many more unknowns and ambiguities than the cooking of food. Still, the overall comparison is useful. A reference librarian is basically a fire-fighter, a generalist, a short-order cook, dishing up cheeseburgers over the counter and whipping up souffles as best he can. A cataloger (or other technical service librarian) has a more limited range of tasks to accomplish, and is under less pressure to accomplish them, at least insofar as he does not have to deal immediately with patron frustration if he postpones basic tasks, so he can concentrate more fully on each task in order to see it through.

Time is of extreme importance in reference work. A discussion during a meeting of the CCS (Cataloging and Classification Section) Heads of Cataloging Departments Discussion Group (at the American Library Association Conference in July 1982) indicates that on the average it takes about an hour to do original cataloging and subject analysis of an item.[9] Imagine what would happen if reference librarians at an ARL library spent an average of an hour each on reference questions. Of course, not all questions need an hour, or even fifteen minutes, but many do, and one of the chief frustrations of reference librarians is that they can hardly afford to spend the ten or fifteen minutes which so many questions really merit, because to do so they would have to leave their colleagues (if there are any) alone to bear the entire burden of ringing telephones, pressuring patrons, and whatever else happens to be transpiring at the desk. If there is no one else on duty, reference librarians are even more reluctant to go off for extended periods of time, knowing as they do that many tentative patrons will not wait at an unstaffed post, and need to be reassured that yes, this *is* the reference desk, it *is* staffed, and we *will* eventually be able to give you some help, although perhaps not as much as you really need, or as much as we would like to give you.

What typically happens to new reference librarians, and to reference librarians who go to large universities from small colleges or public libraries, is that they entertain their first difficult reference questions with energy and enthusiasm, and set off on a fifteen or thirty-minute quest for answers. They return to the obvious disgruntlement of colleagues who have been left to cope with the flood, and they see the blinking phone lights and the line-up of patrons. After a short while, they learn how to give cursory help, to take initial questions at face value rather than probe, and to dump patrons off at the nearest likely index or catalog drawer. The phenomenon I have just described is responsible for much of the shipshod reference service which House and others have criticized,[10] and the ill-effects of time pressure on good reference service is a serious problem which we must address at some point, though it is beyond the scope of this paper. The immediate point is that, for better or worse, reference questions can be handled quickly if not with good qualitative results, and the number of questions handled can be increased by factors of one hundred percent, provided that we are willing to frazzle the brains of reference librarians, give short shrift to more patrons, and lower the overall quality of what is done at the desk. If results are bad, the impact will be limited in most cases to individual patrons who have low expectations to begin with and may not even realize that they have been short-changed.

Cataloging, on the other hand, is literally open to public display on the cathode ray tube; there is a blacklist, and there are lasting consequences when work is poorly done. Quality control becomes of prime importance when a record is made to last forever and be used by hundreds of libraries. In order to assure quality, a whole sequence of clerical and professional tasks needs to be done, authority records and catalogs need to be checked, and the whole process requires that the object under consideration "be seen steadily and whole,"[11] and be worked with through to a satisfactory conclusion. It seems highly unlikely, therefore, that we will be able to do away with technical service departments, as Michael Gorman has suggested.[12] Unless all cataloging is derived, all ordering is automatic, and all other processing functions and record-keeping are eliminated, we will continue to need contemplative places which are untouched by the madding crowd, and which allow librarians, like French chefs, to create their soup-to-nuts specialties.

The nature of reference work is more eclectic, and most reference librarians will never learn to be French chefs. This does not mean, however, that it would not behoove them to know as much as possible about the cuisine of technical processing. Lack of such knowledge is surely a major cause of less-than-excellent reference work. We have no way of knowing how many reference questions have been flubbed as a result of a lack of knowledge of the catalog, of the collection, or of the other technical and clerical processes which become so important when one serves as the interface between the users and the processes. As Murray Martin puts it,

> Reference and circulation librarians have . . . separated service from its organizational basis by fragmenting their activities. In general, education they receive lacks the depth of

knowledge of bibliographic systems, including cataloging, which is required to utilize the resources of the whole library. (p. 85)

I suspect that the need to help create circulation databases compatible with cataloging records has moved circulation librarians much closer to the organizational basis to which Martin refers, but reference librarians have not had to move closer to the center, despite the obvious benefit that such movement would have on good reference work.

One or two cataloging courses in library school do not make a cataloger, and knowledge not worked with on a daily basis fades. Moreover, nothing in library school can prepare reference librarians for the maze of clerical processes which makes the back room into a mysterious black box. Works enter it naked, and emerge fully cataloged and processed, but no one in reference could really say exactly how this comes about. And cataloging rules change all the time. My most recent issue of *American Libraries* announces the publication of nineteen revisions to AACR2, which "are available on loose sheets for insertion into volumes already purchased."[13] I doubt that many reference librarians own the basic volumes, and I doubt that many reference librarians will soon see these loose sheets or be aware of the changes they represent. We think we're doing well when we work with the ninth edition of *Library of Congress Subject Headings*, even though this incorporates changes only up through 1978. It takes a cataloger who sits on our Freshman Workbook revision committee to tell us that a question will no longer work because we do not use that heading any more, just as it takes a clerk to track down an uncataloged Ph.D. thesis somewhere in process, and a bibliographer to tell us, much to our embarrassment, that a particular reference book already in our collection will answer the question we ask him.

It is not surprising that reference librarians may not have a thorough grasp of AACR2, that they do not negotiate the paper trails in the processing jungles, or that they do not have as in-depth a knowledge of a subject as a particular bibliographer may have. All librarians are specialists in certain activities, and reference librarians can do many things which other people know little about. Even within reference librarianship, there are many special activities – instruction, database searching, and interlibrary loan, for instance. In addition, there are subject areas of specialization (education, law, literature, chemistry), and specializations by kinds of materials, such as government documents. No one will ever master all the areas within reference which he would like to know, and it is much less likely that any reference librarian will ever master technical services librarianship. Gorman's ideal of vertical integration, in which the same person performs "all appropriate professional functions" in a subject area, "including selection, collection development, reader advisory and reference services, original cataloging (when copy is not available), and bibliographic instruction"[14] sounds like bibliographic heaven to me, a situation devoutly to be wished for but unlikely to be realized except in special libraries. Even if we eliminated committee work, professional association activities, compensatory time off for working evenings and weekends, vacations, and sick time, there would still be too few hours in the day, and there is still too much specialized knowledge involved for one person to be able to do so many things. There is an economy of scale achieved through specialization, and the disasters which would result if everyone did everything in vertical integration in a large university library are more the stuff of comic fiction than of serious inquiry.

Still, the intent is laudable, and a modified version of Gorman's proposal might very well work. There is no good reason, for instance, for reference librarians to engage in descriptive cataloging, but it makes a good deal of sense for them to assign subject headings. It makes no sense for reference librarians to do clerical work in the acquisitions area, but there are very good reasons why every reference librarian should have a good knowledge of the entire sequence of materials processing, and they should all be walked through this process until they feel comfortable with it. Reference librarians may not have the time to do all of the selection for a particular area of the general collection, along with weeding, binding decisions, and the other aspects of collection development associated with it, but there are very good reasons why reference librarians should be sitting in on meetings of the bibliographers in order to learn about what is happening to the general collection.

In addition to the role of reference librarians as interpreters of the general collection, and the importance of a knowledge of cataloging in that regard, reference librarians also have their own collection to acquire and manage, and as they go about caring for a reference collection a knowledge of acquisitions and collection development techniques is equally important. Collection management is hardly a minor activity in reference departments. Most large reference departments have spent considerable time formulating collection development policies and spend much time on a continuing basis on matters such as ordering, weeding, and binding.[15] In doing so they are interacting constantly with the general library environment and with its technical processes, and the person in charge of the collection had better understand those processes well and, in addition, have a good working relationship with the library's bibliographers. These people, in many cases, exercise veto power over reference orders, which can sometimes create bad feelings but which may also be a good discipline which forces the reference librarian to articulate why particular purchases are necessary. Sometimes a particular item may already exist elsewhere in the library in different form, or it may not be a cost-effective purchase given the curricular needs of the students. Interplay between reference librarians and bibliographers is crucial in determining how valuable the reference collection itself will be in the future.

Still, reference librarians must also be their own bibliographers. Selection in most large reference departments is a group rather than an individual activity. A selection committee meets regularly to propose and approve orders. This may be a committee with rotating members or, as in my situation, it may be a standing committee of the whole. Reference librarians bring their various subject and language specialties to the selection meetings, and should also work closely with the library's bibliographer in that area to assure that appropriate materials are known to each and ordered for the right places. Reference selection is greatly facilitated, by the way, if the department maintains in-process records of what it currently has on order and what has recently arrived. In this way, much time is saved because reference librarians do not spend time discussing items they have already ordered or received, nor do the library's searching people need to waste time on these items. Needless to say, the advent of online in-process files and the amalgamation of these files into circulation and cataloging files should obviate the need for this tiresome searching and maintenance of manual records.

Selection committee meetings are most fruitful if reference librarians have been able to search orders thoroughly and consider them in the total context of the reference collection. Just as a search of the library's order file may reveal that the item has already been ordered for some other collection, which may necessitate a second-copy decision, a search of OCLC may well reveal that the item is in fact a reprint of an ERIC document or a government document which the library already has and which need not be duplicated at all. Nor should selection decisions be limited to the question of whether or not the library has an item. There are also intellectual decisions to be made about whether or not the reference collection needs an item. Here reference librarians need to consider the nature of their institutions, as well as of their budgets, and they need to weigh the relative value of acquisitions. In this regard, comparative reviews such as those published by *Choice* are particularly useful, but even these are only a partial guide. I have ordered works described as "useless" in *Choice* reviews, and found these items quite useful in my library. Reference librarians must ultimately choose those works which they know will be useful to them and to their patrons, and no review can really provide sufficient context in which to make selection decisions.

Approximately one book truck full of new items is added every week to my reference room which, like most reference rooms, is finite in size, and needs to be weeded as it grows and as items lose their current reference value. If you have ever spearheaded the weeding of 5,000 items from a 50,000 volume reference collection, as I have, you know the necessity of working closely with technical services people, probably to your chagrin, and definitely to their sorrow. You cannot send books off to the stacks blithely without deprogramming them and altering their reference location identities. Room has to be made on shelves somewhere else for the departing books; slips have to be filled out properly, and shelf list records pulled, so that cataloging and circulation records can be changed. And when you make an error, as you inevitably do, and weed something which should have been kept, you must suffer the slings and arrows of faculty members and catalog maintenance people and bibliographers as you reverse the process, restamp the books "Reference," and make room for them again on your own shelves.

Throughout this paper I have used the relationship between reference and technical services as a focal point for describing reference work because I believe that closer interaction between the various areas of librarianship is the wave of the future. For proof of this contention, one need turn no further than to the September 1982 issue of *American Libraries*. In the job ads section, the following advertisement for an Associate Director for Public Services describes the position thus:

> Coordinates public services activities with technical services and special collections divisions. Works with collection development officer; works with library systems division in implementation of an integrated automated library system. (p. 517)

Clearly, those who hope to enter reference or any public service work in the future will have to have a more integrated view of librarianship than has been necessary in recent years. The databases used by reference librarians will eventually be the same ones used by the technical services people – not only OCLC, RLIN, and WLN, but also USBE, Books in Print, Ulrich's, CULP, and REMARC. When people look back at reference service in ten or twenty years, they will see today as the end of an era. There was a time when machines were not impotant and when reference librarians really did not need to know anything about them in order to do good work. That time is past. There was a time, also, when student enrollments were rising, and librarians of any kind were hard to find. That time is past too.

Reference librarians can no longer afford to be defenders of an outmoded tradition which disdainfully eschews such things as library instruction and automation, and sees reference librarianship as a guild separate from the cataloger's guild, the bibliographer's guild, and the other guilds. We may not know as much about other areas of librarianship as those who work with them full time, but we must know as much about them as we reasonably can in order to do our own jobs well. Those who are not willing to expand their conception of librarianship and are not willing to take a systems approach to the mission of their libraries will, more and more, hinder the accomplishment of that mission.

A library is a seamless and indivisible system, not a collection of snap-on parts. A library is a living organism which cannot function well unless the functions interact and support each other. The biggest waste of a university's resources is to have a library with an enormous technical services operation buying and cataloging materials, storing them in expensive buildings, churning out catalog cards or online records of various kinds — all of which are little used because people cannot find them or are not aware that they might even be there. The fact is that technical service people need reference people to actualize the potential of what they are creating, just as reference people depend on technical services people to create the environment in which help becomes possible to give.

The need to narrow the distance between reference and technical services works both ways, however. Catalogers and bibliographers not only need to use reference tools in their work but also have to know what the library's patrons need and how they go about finding it. With this knowledge, technical service librarians can go about their subject cataloging, acquisitions, and selection activities more effectively. Still, it would be as impractical for them to spend large amounts of time doing reference work as it would be for reference librarians to devote large amounts of time to cataloging and general library acquisitions.

Given the practical barriers which separate them, how might we nevertheless increase contact between reference and technical service librarians for their mutual benefit? The first thing which comes to mind is library education. Library school is probably not the place to encourage specialization, which will occur soon enough anyway, and which cannot be mastered in a one-year MLS program. Students should be encouraged to see the connections which underlie all library work, and they should be discouraged from identifying themselves too quickly as reference librarians or as any other kind of librarians. They should be exposed to as varied a course structure as possible.

While broader library education efforts would help, however, they would not be enough, and students will soon forget the details they have learned. Moreover, technical service procedures differ so much from library to library that no library school education could prepare students to follow the procedures of particular institutions. Therefore, we need a continuing education system which brings all librarians into closer contact with their institution's work processes and with new developments in the profession. We need to encourage professional associations to put on substantive programs, and we need to encourage libraries to initiate or expand staff development efforts which bring various areas into contact with each other.

Finally, we need to expand formal opportunities for communication between departments within libraries. This expansion is probably more important for the indians on the staff than it is for the chiefs who are usually forced to communicate at some point. But the average reference librarian rarely has a chance to interact professionally with catalogers, and catalogers rarely help to make decisions about reference matters. This lack of communication could be addressed by making sure that there is better library-wide representation in our various efforts. For instance, catalogers and reference librarians can jointly give library instruction sessions on how to use OCLC, and technical services people can generally be involved in library instruction efforts at minimal cost of their time. Similarly, reference and other public service people should be attending the meetings of cataloging and bibliography departments, not only to find out what is going on, but also to add their knowledge to the pool for our mutual benefit. Exchange of staff meeting minutes is another quick and efficient way to expand knowledge of activities in other areas of the library.

These solutions are partial and imperfect, but then so are library systems in general. The thing to do is not to throw up one's hands, but rather to look for ways to ameliorate the problem. We have only just begun to think about the problem of integrating reference into the environment of technical services more fully, and there is clearly much that can be accomplished in the near future with a modicum of effort.[16]

NOTES

1. Williams A. Katz, *Introduction to Reference Work, Volume I: Basic Information Sources*, 4th ed. (New York: McGraw-Hill, 1982), p. 3.

2. Donald Davinson, *Reference Service* (London: Clive Bingley, 1980), p. 11.

3. Jay Bausser, "Online Catalogs," *RTSD Newsletter* 7:17 (March-April, 1982).

4. Diana M. Thomas. Ann T. Hinckley, and Elizabeth R. Eisenbach, *The Effective Reference Librarian* (New York: Academic Press, 1981), p. 192.

5. Ibid.

6. Betsy Baker and Kathleen Kluegel, "Availability and Use of OCLC for Reference in Large Academic Libraries," *RQ* 21: 379–83 (Summer 1982).
   There is no need to be afraid of putting OCLC terminals out for public use; my experience is that people take to it with surprising ease. The public searching instructions created by several members of my department will soon be available through ERIC; until they are, I would be happy to provide copies for interested libraries.

7. It is of course difficult to generalize about the nature of work at reference desks because some schools have divisional arrangements, some serve fewer undergraduates, and some do not serve the public. Here I consider the worst-case situation (which happens also to be my own) — generous amounts of every kind of patron and a wide diversity of questions. Even in such situations, of course, there are quieter times, especially between terms.

8. For a good discussion of this problem, see David S. Ferriero and Kathleen A. Powers, "Burnout at the Reference Desk," *RQ* 21:274–79 (Spring 1982).

9. Beacher J. Wiggins, "CCS Heads of Cataloging Departments Discussion Group," *Library of Congress Information Bulletin* 41:243 (August 13, 1982).

10. David E. House, "Reference Efficiency or Reference Deficiency," *Library Association Record* 76:222–23 (November 1972).
    This article is reprinted in *Reference and Information Services: A Reader*, edited by Bill Katz and Andrea Tarr (Metuchen, NJ: Scarecrow Press, 1978), pp. 140–44. Other recent studies which found disappointing performance at reference desks include Egill Halldorssen and Marjorie Murfin, "The Performance of Professionals and Nonprofessionals in the Reference Interview," *College & Research Libraries* 38:385–95 (September

1977), and John P. Wilkinson and William Miller, "The Step Approach to Reference Service," *RQ* 17:293–300 (Summer 1978).

11. Murray S. Martin, *Issues in Personnel Management in Academic Libraries* (Greenwich, CT: JAI, 1981), p. 201.
    Further quotation from this book is cited in the text.

12. See Gorman's article "On Doing Away with Technical Services Departments" in *American Libraries* 10:435–37 (July-August, 1979).

13. "AACR2 Revisions," *American Libraries* 13:546 (September 1982).
    Further quotation from this issue is cited in the text.

14. Gorman, 436–37.

15. At the 1982 meeting of the RASD Reference Services in Large Research Libraries Discussion Group (during ALA in Philadelphia) a show of hands revealed that a majority of the departments represented were actively engaged in various collection development activities, including the formulation of written policies.

16. Those interested in pursuing this topic should also read the short and humorous article by Edward J. Bachus, "The Integration of Technical and Reader Services," *JAL* 8:227+260 (September 1982); unfortunately I did not receive this issue in time to incorporate Bachus' article into my text.

Professional Attitudes, Productive Roles:
Roads to Achievement

Keith M. Cottam

One day nearly thirteen years ago I was picking up the morning mail when a colleague stopped me and blurted out something that has left me with a lasting impression. His voice was tinged with a certain tone of frustration: "How do you do it; I mean, how do you manage to get everything done? You've got a family, you're involved in church and the Utah Library Association, you're getting things published, and you seem to be succeeding around here. What is it...."

His voice trailed off and I stood there a bit awkwardly for a moment, more embarrassed than flattered by the inquiry. I do not remember exactly what I said, only that I mumbled something about organizing my time, setting priorities and loving my work; not a very worthy response for the impulsive but serious nature of the inquiry. I walked away from the encounter very reflective, filled with introspection about my personal and professional life; about what it is that makes people rise above the norm; about the abilities required for me and others to succeed; about knowledge, skills, attitudes and roles — about why and how we achieve.

Motivation and Achievement

Achievement is an elusive yet essential, indefinable yet recognizable quality of life that haunts us all at one time or another. We worry about providing for family needs, raising our standard of living, and coping with the responsibility of children, church and community life. Yesterday we worried about our performance evaluation. Today you receive a rejection slip from an editor. Tonight you meet with the school board. Tomorrow we must work at the reference desk, compile a bibliographic guide for a class of graduate students, and gather our wits to give a lecture before a classroom of unfamiliar undergraduate faces. Next year: the kids are growing older, we thing we should test the job market, and we will worry about a pay raise, the bottom line for most of us and a measure of how much we are worth.

You are probably aware that a multimillion-dollar industry has grown from our need to achieve and succeed. Dale Carnegie, Paul Myer, Napoleon Hill, Og Mandino, Maxwell Maltz and David Schwartz are but a few of the big names on the popular front of the achievement or motivation field.

On the scholarly side are authorities such as Abraham Maslow, whose "Hierarchy of Human Needs" is the base on which most modern motivation theory is built.[1] He postulated that as individuals we move up in the hierarchy from physical needs to safety or security needs, then to social belonging, on to esteem or what others think of us, and finally to some kind of self-actualization or feeling that we are making the most of ourselves.

Frederick Herzberg's book, *Work and the Nature of Man*, introduced his "Motivation-Hygiene" theory to wide attention in 1966.[2] Herzberg's "Motivation" needs are directly associated with a person's tasks and include challenging work, achievement, recognition, increasing responsibility and the opportunity to grow and develop. His "Hygiene" needs are not task-related, but are a part of the environment in which the work is done, such as supervision, policies, working conditions, interpersonal relationships, security, status and money. According to Herzberg, improving "Hygiene" factors will reduce dissatisfaction but will not motivate. Improving "Hygiene" factors as well as enriching a job, such as offering more challenge, paving the way for achievement, giving recognition, delegating responsibility and allowing growth, will lead to a higher level of motivation.

David McClelland, an eminent psychologist known for his research on competencies and achievement motives, says the achievement drive is a "learned motivation." We are not born with it, and only about ten percent of the U.S. population can be called achievers. Achievement is best learned on a job where an individual can assume more responsibility; participate personally in goal setting; establish high but not impossible goals; receive fast, clearcut feedback; and get frank, detailed performance evaluation.[3]

And so the issue of motivation, with all its variations and angles "guaranteed" to place you on the road to personal achievement and success, is intriguing. The field spawns much diverse but related study and comment, and the charismatic showmen of the popular movement can literally sweep you up, mind and soul, into thinking bigger, believing more fervently, organizing efficiently and moving out ahead of the pack. The slogans are themselves captivating, if not downright exciting:

"Get the action habit!" (Schwartz)

"The secret of success is goal setting!" (Myer)

"Think and grow rich!" (Hill)

"Win friends and influence people!" (Carnegie)

"Attain a positive image!" (Maltz)

And where do librarians fit with all this? How many of us are among the ten percent who are achievers? Do we apply Maslow or listen to Carnegie? Do we believe in ourselves and have a positive self image? Do we organize our lives as well as we organize our collections? Are we more talk and less action? Do we exercise self-control and the capacity for creativity in solving problems?" Are we self-starters, self-directed and properly motivated?

Perhaps my friend at the mailbox was groping through a similar maze of questions and didn't know where to find the road out. Small wonder, since the nature of what we call the library profession, and what we think is expected of us as professionals, seems fraught with a quagmire-like quality much of the time.

Professional Attitudes

In that observation there is another elusive concept that means many things to many people. Professionalism: One of the biggest issues of our time for librarans. In a lengthy *Library Trends* article in 1978, Lester Asheim examined the shift in attitude during the 1950s, 60s and 70s among librarians in their outlook toward professional status.[4] In a unique study of librarians and their work, William Reeves, a Canadian sociologist, sought to determine circumstances and conditions that lead to or enhance occupational control in an organizational work setting.[5] An example of an alternative to the sociological model of a profession for librarians was published in 1975 by Gardner Hanks and James Schmidt.[6] Millicent Abell, speaking at the ACRL National Conference in Boston, reflected on librarians' ability to escape a working pattern of routine and reaction and to master the professional role.[7] And lest you dismiss the professionalism issue as congenial debate or benign rhetoric, read "Professionalism Under Attack" by Pauline Wilson in the November 1981 issue of *Journal of Academic Librarianship*.

I, too, have contributed my opinion to the discussion in letters-to-the-editor columns, staff documents on faculty status, and in a recent administrative position paper on professionalism, from which

I quote a brief passage:

> "This role perception has fostered certain traditions among academic librarians here and elsewhere, notably that they believe they are educated to do a job, to do it in the absence of unreasonable organizational fetters, and with professional control over the quality and productivity of the entire job. A professionally oriented academic librarian has come to expect to look beyond the confines of a prescribed position and to feel responsibility for raising the organizational vision, showing new opportunities, looking at new horizons, and suggesting new and more demanding standards. If this does not occur, the librarian may be considered a technician."

One can imagine how that last sentence of the statement has been accepted by some members of my "professional-exempt" staff, librarians without faculty status who are striving for an identity on campus.

In the April 1975 issue of *American Libraries* there appeared a "Statement on Professional Ethics, 1975." By June 1979 a revised statement was issued, and in 1981 the ALA membership and Council adopted a new statement.[9] The document is significant as it reflects a community perspective on the nature of the profession and implies qualifications required of librarians. According to the statement: We "influence or control the selection, organization, preservation, and dissemination of information." We are "explicitly committed to intellectual freedom and the freedom of access to information." We "ensure the free flow of information and ideas to present and future generations." We "have obligations for maintaining the highest level of personal integrity and competence."

From those ideals could be drawn a formidable array of specific qualifications for us to meet, yet that is not the way the statement is normally used. In fact, the statement itself is not even frequently cited.

So, the concept of professionalism receives persistent attention in speeches, articles, and books, but the debate is dominated by more philosophy than action, more mental gymnastics than visible productivity. We go to such extraordinary lengths to convince ourselves through public discussion that we are professional, that time and opportunity to *do* something productive usually escapes us. Despite the satisfaction we may get from debating, we realize very little, if any, demonstration of our abilities as professionals. The debate may be a logical exercise, but the arguments too often go nowhere.

Whether or not we keep up with the debate, which seems inevitable, imprecise and subjective, the issue permeates our professional lives. Role, function, status, salary — achievement — all seem imbedded in this fascinating matter.

Competencies and Productive Roles

David McClelland, mentioned above, has also done some interesting work on another concept, the issue of competencies, which has also become a matter significant to my thinking since that day at the mailboxes. McClelland defines "competence" in a special way, not as "aspects of a job but rather characteristics of the people who do the job best. A job-task analysis can break down the specific tasks needed for a job, but that tells you nothing about competencies," or the motives, traits and special skills and abilities which determine the outstanding performers.[10]

Competency-based education, perhaps more familiar, is the root of this topic. Pulled by the forces demanding basic education and accountability, it has risen like a tide in this country. Many states have passed legislation requiring some form of minimum standard testing to be carried out by the schools. While the current has reached all the way to a number of graduate library schools, the single most critical challenge to the effective use of competencies at any level of education is the lack of validation and the instrumentation and processes to measure them. Logically and theoretically, competency-based education and the use of competencies makes sense, but there has grown much controversy over using them in education or the job market.

You may remember when the California Library Selection Project released the infamous list of 36 essential requirements, or competencies, for the "day-one" entry-level librarian. According to a *Library Journal* report, "These required skills indicate that California libraries are looking for the cream of the crop — top-notch beginning librarians capable of performing a wide variety of library tasks — often more than many a seasoned librarian is asked to do."[11]

You may also be familiar with the work of the American Library Association, Office for Library Personnel Resources Minimum Qualifications for Librarians Task Force, which published a report in the May 1980 issue of *American Libraries.*[12] I quote one paragraph from that document:

> "The challenge has arisen: What does a librarian do and what competencies are required for performing a 'professional' job? Does the MLS by current standards meet job competency requirements? How do we ensure that standards

for professional competencies are met when alternative professional career routes are used? Can the MLS as an ideal educational credential withstand legal challenges?"

In another statement, the Task Force observed:

"More research is needed to identify basic competencies needed in librarianship and to determine whether these are met by 'MLS' programs or if they may also be acquired through experience equivalencies or some combination of experience and other academic credentials. The Task Force recognizes that some library systems wish to allow alternative routes to professional positions, but alternative routes must ensure that standards of professional competencies are met so that the public interest will be protected. If alternative qualifications to the 'MLS' are adopted by libraries, the Task Force now recommends that the related selection procedures be carefully validated to ensure that the applicants possess the necessary competencies. Because professional validation is a highly technical, expensive and time-consuming procedure, alternative qualifications should not be established arbitrarily or hastily."[13]

While the profession at large has paid little attention to the MQ issue, except as libraries and librarians become the focus of civil service, affirmative action or Equal Opportunity challenges, there does exist concern in several places. The U.S. Department of Education recently released a Request for Proposal in anticipation of "awarding a contract of 18 months duration in order to identify the present and future competencies needed by library and information science professionals. The contract will also examine the education requirements necessary to achieve those competencies."[14]

The Office for Library Personnel Resources of the American Library Association has prepared a grant proposal, unrelated to the U.S. Department of Education RFP, and is seeking funding to conduct a job analysis study for librarian positions. The purpose of the study would be to determine the functions of a librarian's job and to examine the skills, knowledge, abilities and personal characteristics which are required for successful professional job performance.

And in a move vigorously resisted by the library community, the U.S. Office of Personnel Management proposed on December 8, 1981, new classification and qualification standards for federal librarians and technical information specialists. The proposed standards have implications not only for federal librarians but also may influence positions in other types of libraries, as well as education for the profession.[15]

Roads to Achievement: Personal Choices

But what is the most important ingredient for achievement? What aspects of professionalism are critical for success? What are the competencies, the characteristics, the skills, abilities and knowledge that will help to distinguish the super-stars from the mediocre performers? I draw on the wisdom of Robert Frost to direct our attention away from generalizations about motivation and achievement, qualifications and competencies, and toward some specific suggestions.

THE ROAD NOT TAKEN

Two roads diverged in a yellow wood,
And sorry I could not travel both
And be one traveler, long I stood
And looked down one as far as I could
To where it bent in the undergrowth;

Then took the other, as just as fair,
And having perhaps the better claim,
Because it was grassy and wanted wear;
Though as for that the passing there
Had worn them really about the same,

And both that morning equally lay
In leaves no step had trodden black.
Oh, I kept the first for another day!
Yet knowing how way leads on to way,
I doubted if I should ever come back.

I shall be telling this with a sigh
Somewhere ages and ages hence:
Two roads diverged in a wood and I —
I took the one less traveled by,
And that has made all the difference.

So it goes. In order to be different, in order to achieve and make an impact on the quality of our lives and the quality of the institutions in which we serve, we must be prepared to take a road not traveled by the majority. One must exercise some distinct and uncommon behaviors: imagination, initiative, individuality, independence, commitment, action and sacrifice.

At the January 1982 conference of the Association of American Library Schools, Patricia Battin and Margot McBurney, responding to the educators' interest in "what library directors want" when they hire new professionals, described several qualities. Ms. Battin suggested four basic personal qualifications:

> "1) A first-rate mind with problem-solving abilities ... is non-negotiable.... 2) A solid undergraduate preparation in any of a variety of disciplines: the key is the rigor of the training, not the subject discipline.... 3) Concrete evidence of managerial abilities: almost every research library responsibility, even at the entry level, now requires some degree of sophisticated management of either people or resources .... 4) An intellectual commitment to research librarianship...."[16]

She also noted the need for a "specially designed set of qualifications and rigorous educational preparation," the need for education "for a life-long career as opposed to vocational training," and the "need for people who welcome the challenge ... and who are prepared to take the risks involved."

Ms. McBurney explained that "Research library professionals should be comfortable in an online environment and well-grounded in managing technical operations (which are 'the first public service') as well as in reference services. They need preparation in budgeting, planning, labor relations, personnel, and organization development."[17]

Elizabeth Stone, the immediate past president of the American Library Association, published a study in 1969 which is still relevant.[18] Her findings, based on the qualifications of librarians and what motivates or deters them from professional development activities, pointed explicitly to the need for *action on the part of individuals*. The findings in her "Conclusions and Recommendations"

> "... showed a significant disparity between what the librarians were doing and what they thought they should be doing for maximum professional development. The entire sample seemed to regard activities that were somewhat informal and which provided social contacts with other professionals as more important. These were also the activities in which they were most involved. The librarians were less involved with activities which call for independent action. Most of their time was devoted to library association work; meetings and conventions; visiting other libraries; recruiting

for the profession; and reading professional literature, particularly library journals."

The data from the study showed very poor participation in the areas of research, publication, delivery of papers at professional meetings, reading in non-library professional journals, membership in learned societies and non-library professional associations. Further, librarians reported relatively low concern for the problems of fellow workers on and off the job, and very few had a personal plan for further study and professional development.

I suspect that if the study were repeated today there would be little difference in the results, except that we are not concerned about shortages of librarians and we are more aware of the need for continuing education.

Now, saying all this there is a tendency in listening to expert opinions, studying the research or reading the literature, to find it impersonal and remote from the struggles we all face. A few examples serve to illustrate the perspective of personal lives, mine and those of a few colleagues who are willing to share their experience.

People

You cannot be good in the library business, particularly with reference services, unless you are sensitive to other people: uninformed students, arrogant faculty members, troubled staff colleagues, irate telephone callers, people who are okay and those who are not — all of them are part of our world. If we start from the premise that basic courtesy and respect are essential, we can move from there to sharpen our human relations skills, reference interview techniques and organizational effectiveness. There is a wealth of published material available about human behavior. Draw upon it.

Draw also upon inspiration from your colleagues. I am convinced that job satisfaction and professional success are fostered through a process of formal and informal communication; and on the basis of valuable, continued, and close interaction with particular individuals. History has shown that since the time of Mentor, close friend of the Greek king Odysseus and the trusted guardian of the king's son Telemachus, a great mind is almost always the result of time spent with another good mind, that exceptional teachers produce exceptional students. Facts may be learned from books, experience from life, but a passion for ideas and the ability to create with them is an enthusiasm caught from others. Mentors not only help their students find the pieces, they often also work with students in putting together the puzzle.

Marvin Wiggins, an outstanding person and reference librarian at Brigham Young University, states: "I find that my contacts with people are frequently more valuable than what I learn through professional literature. Most invitations to publish and speak were a result of my consultation with other professional librarians. I feel that my success is proportionately related to the success I can help others have."[19]

And Eugene Sheehy, Head of the Reference Department at Columbia University and editor of the *Guide to Reference Books*, notes that he "was fortunate in the people who taught (him) bibliographic method," and "not surprisingly, Constance M. Winchell is the person who has most influenced (his) career."[20]

Pat Swanson, the eminently successful Head of Reference Services at the University of Chicago, recognizes three people who have been particularly important in her life.

> "All are strong women who made no apologies for being librarians, who stressed quality in work and who believed that librarians are important to the academic enterprise. These women are Caroline T. Spicer, Loda M. Hopkins, and Christine Reb Longstreet. Yet, I am not like any of these three women and I suppose *that* is the most valuable lesson I learned from them. Each set high standards for me, but none expected me to be a carbon copy of her. I could pursue my different interests, hold different opinions and still be highly regarded. I hope I have taken this lesson to heart in working with younger colleagues and think that it has contributed to my success."[21]

Larry Earl Bone, Director of Libraries at Mercy College, writes of an earlier experience:

> "Going to Illinois was certainly the most important and fortunate professional move I made. I was given tremendous professional opportunity there. Both Herbert Goldhor and Robert Downs gave me the utmost encouragement and many professional opportunities."[22]

While ability and skill with people relationships are the most important elements in our inventory of qualifications, we cannot spend our lives in activities which are somewhat informal and which provide only social contacts. We must place in our lives a framework of personal values, institutional foundations and orderly structures which will support our pursuit of excellence.

Planning

Planning, for example, is nearly always acknowledged as an essential part of our lives, but it is commonly sidestepped or accomplished irregularly and with questionable results. In a recent *RQ* article, I observed:

> "My experience for eight years as a reference librarian, and for nearly ten years now as an administrator, confirms that conclusion. As a reference librarian I was eager and intent about doing my job, about getting on with the action. I was impatient and in a hurry, and planning was frequently overlooked; but as an administrator I am aware that planning is essential in order to give direction and credibility to doing a job. I have learned that I must be both a planner and a doer. From planning come better design and more responsive programs. Planning clarifies needs, goals, objectives, procedures, and methods, and it paves the way for evaluation and improvement."[23]

In view of the time required to place order in our lives through planning, I am not surprised when librarians tell me they give little formal attention to the task. But the degree of our success in using our time wisely and productively is governed by how carefully we plan.

Marvin Wiggins again:

> "I learned . . . that if my career was to be stimulating and productive, it would be up to me to create that situation. By pulling together the ideas from the Instructional Development Department, educational psychologists, content experts from academic departments who use library instruction, educational media experts, electronic engineers, and by tapping into ideas from leaders in the library profession, we could build a program based on sound philosophical principles with proven results that would meet the needs of our university community."

And Eugene Sheehy: "I have considerable capacity for organization (and accomplishment) of work and for attention to detail," absolute necessities for successful planning.

Larry Bone observes the need for a "strong belief in the necessity for understanding clearly an institution's mission before pursuing its activities," a critical first factor if you expect to have a productive planning process.

Productivity

Productive librarians also realize the degree of achievement is dependent on the level to which planning and goals are carried, and on the intensity of the commitment to achieve. We make choices, deciding what is important for us to do and accomplish. We are forced to focus on the important or priority concerns first, and sometimes success seems a long way off. For most of us, in fact, we work for years for a little success, a little visibility. But I suggest that we should take a reasonable amount of time, time to grasp conceptual ability as well as technical knowledge, time to observe and listen and learn, time to distinguish between needs and wants, and time to think through the investments in time and energy required for productivity in view of personal values and priorities. The achievement, the status we seek, will come in that context of appropriate design.

The issue of faculty status will illustrate this point. My feelings on this matter arise from the fact that status is of two kinds. Objective status, that which is granted by an institution, comes out of conditions which the institution controls. It is granted independent of our actions and will come about only through the willingness of the institution. Subjective status, based on individual planning, perseverance, performance and achievement, is earned and shaped by specific, long-term, professional behavior. We must strengthen our effort to gain subjective status, and, perhaps in time, objective status will follow.

On this matter of productivity, my friends are unusually humble. I assume that as I was at the mailboxes, they are more embarrassed than flattered by the recognition. They play down their accomplishments. They give birth to ideas, solve problems, begin projects and see their publications in print, and then they move quietly to other challenges without fanfare.

Now that I have added more verbiage to the record, I wish to say that my message is really quite simple. If confronted at the mailboxes again, I may talk on a little as I have done here, and offer more personal examples, but in essence I would say that aside from credentials earned through formal education, there are certain competencies, qualifications if you wish, which will give you an edge on achievement. First, learn to define what you want to accomplish in the context of your personal values and aspirations, in view of your responsibilities and obligations, and on the basis of a realistic assessment of your capabilities. I hasten to suggest that most of us tap but a mere fraction of our capabilities, so shoot high in your assessment. Put some energy into these definitions, isolating specifically what goals you want to achieve.

Next, develop a plan for reaching your goals. Establish sound reasons and desires for what you want to do, set deadlines and learn to manage your time as well as your tasks. Plans for human enterprise should be dynamic, always being refined and improved. As new insights occur, take notes to yourself, updating and adjusting your course of action as necessary.

Develop personal confidence in your ability to achieve. Perhaps more than any other reason, we remain mediocre because we fear what we have yet to try. We fear making mistakes, fear rejection, fear taking risks, fear letting colleagues look over our shoulder, and fear being unsuccessful. The fear leads to lack of confidence, indecision, lack of action and poor achievement. Chip away at your reluctance and hesitancy to do more or try more difficult activities. If you don't try, you will never really know what you can achieve.

Finally, Eugene Sheehy says that " 'Perseverance' is the quality that probably has had most to do with [his] professional success." His determination and sustained effort has, of course, produced the famous *Guide to Reference Books*, and while your opportunities may not be as visible, they are no less important for you. For you to stand idle wondering what to do next will lead nowhere; to take to the road, particularly to the more rigorous and less traveled, will make "all the difference."

NOTES

1. Maslow, Abraham. *Motivation and Personality*. 2d ed. New York: Harper & Row, 1970.

2. For a brief perspective on Herzberg's work, see Herzberg, Frederick. "One More Time: How Do You Motivate Employees?" *Harvard Business Review* 46 (January-February 1968): 53–62.

3. McClelland, David D. and David H. Burnham. "Power Is the Great Motivator." *Harvard Business Review* 54 (March-April 1976): 100–110.

4. Asheim, Lester. "Librarians as Professionals." *Library Trends* 26 (Winter 1978): 225–257.

5. Reeves, William Joseph. *Librarians as Professionals*. Lexington, MA: D.C. Heath, 1980.

6. Hanks, Gardner and C. James Schmidt. "An Alternative Model of a Profession for Librarians." *College & Research Libraries* 36 (May 1975): 175–187.

7. Abell, Millicent D. "The Changing Role of the Academic Librarian: Drift and Mastery." *College & Research Libraries* 40 (March 1979): 154–164.

8. Wilson, Pauline. "Professionalism under Attack!" *The Journal of Academic Librarianship* 7 (November 1981): 283–290.

9. "Statement on Professional Ethics, 1981." *ALA Handbook of Organization 1981/1982*, p. 197.

10. Goleman, Daniel. "The New Competency Tests: Matching the Right People to the Right Jobs." *Psychology Today*, January 1981, pp. 35–46.

11. "Californians Peg Entry Level Librarian I 'Tasks.' " *Library Journal*, November 15, 1977, pp. 2298, 2300.

12. Cottam, Keith. "Minimum Qualifications and the Law: The Issue Ticks Away for Librarians." *American Libraries*, May 1980, pp. 280–281.

13. "Minimum Qualifications for Librarians: What Are the Issues?" A question and answer document prepared by the American Library Association, Office for Library Personnel Resources Minimum Qualifications for Librarians Task Force, May 1980.

14. RFP 82–24. U.S. Department of Education, Office of Procurement and Assistance Management, Washington, DC 20202. (NOTE: A contract, No. 300–82–0152, "New Directions in Library and Information Science Education," was awarded through the U.S. Department of Education Office of Libraries and Learning Technologies to King Research, Inc., on September 30, 1982, for approximately $244,000. The period of performance for the grant is September 30, 1982 to March 30, 1984.)

15. See, for example, the report in *Library Journal*, February 1, 1982, pp. 208–209, for background on this issue.

16. Battin, Patricia. "The Real World – Large Library Organizations." A panel presentation at the Association of American Library Schools Annual Conference, January 22, 1982, Denver, Colorado.

17. McBurney, Margot. As reported in the *ARL Newsletter*, No. 110 (March 5, 1982), p. 4.

18. Stone, Elizabeth W. *Factors Related to the Professional Development of Librarians.* New Jersey: Scarecrow Press, 1969.

19. This and further quotes from Mr. Wiggins contained in a letter to the author from Marvin E. Wiggins, August 11, 1982.

20. This and further quotes from Mr. Sheehy contained in a letter to the author from Eugene P. Sheehy, August 9, 1982.

21. Contained in a letter to the author from Patricia Swanson, August 18, 1982.

22. This and further quotes from Mr. Bone contained in a letter to the author from Larry Earl Bone, August 24, 1982.

23. Cottam, Keith M. "Avoiding Failure: Planning User Education." *RQ* 21 (Summer 1982): 331–333.

"The Road Not Taken," by Robert Frost, taken from the author's personal file.

The Widening Gyre:
Resource Sharing and Its Impact on Reference Services

Sheila Dowd

My title is taken from a poem whose apocalyptic note has made it much quoted in our times. The poem is Yeats' "The Second Coming," which begins:

> Turning and turning in the widening gyre
> The falcon cannot hear the falconer;
> Things fall apart; the centre cannot hold;
> Mere anarchy is loosed upon the world . . . .[1]

In thinking about libraries, networks and resource sharing, the lines seem relevant to me.

The "widening gyre" of library services, the outward- and upward-spiraling patterns of interdependence, the commitments we are all making to cooperative service and mutual reliance — this movement outward can place a strain upon the "centre," the individual library. Our challenge is to assure that the widening commitments do not move the library beyond the call of its clients; but rather, enable it to heed and serve them better.

It is appropriate to speak of these problems to reference librarians. We who provide the library's front-line services are the users' confidants (and sometimes their scapegoats or whipping-boys) when they have problems in using the library. We are charged with responsibility for being their advocates in library planning. To speak of the impact of resource sharing on reference services is in fact to speak of its impact on library users and library use. Reference librarians are in an ideal position to help library administrators assess the real value of cooperative programs, their costs and benefits to users; and to ensure that cooperation results in enhancement of service, not "mere anarchy" loosed upon our libraries.

Allow me first, for the sake of clarity, to define "reference services" and "resource sharing." By "reference services" I mean the complex of informational, bibliographic and instructional services we provide to help library clients find their way through recorded knowledge to satisfy their scholarly or informational needs.

The term "resource sharing" covers a wide range of cooperative activities between libraries. In considering the impact of resource sharing on reference services we will look at developments in bibliographic access, in information and bibliographic services, in physical access services and in cooperative collection development. I like this broad definition which covers the whole range of activities to be discussed: "Basically, resource sharing is used here to refer to the generic process by which information or human services at one library are made available to another to meet user needs at a remote location."[2]

In approaching these large topics, I would like to give you a brief overview of the history of cooperative efforts. Then I will discuss the substantive areas mentioned before (bibliographic access, information and bibliographic servics, physical access services, and cooperative collection development) and examine the impact of each on reference services. Finally, I will conclude with a little advice about expectations from resource sharing and evaluation of programs.

History

Cooperative efforts have a long history in American libraries. David Weber provides an interesting survey in his article, "A Century of Cooperative Programs among Academic Libraries."[3] He cites a number of early ventures in cooperation. There were efforts toward cooperative cataloging in New York State as early as the 1870s. In 1898 Joseph Rowell, the first University of California librarian, offered to lend to those libraries which would lend to UC. (I must investigate this further; does Berkeley perhaps bear responsibility for the creation of that Frankenstein's monster, interlibrary loan?) Lowell Martin notes[4] that by February 1913 the *Library Journal* was carrying an article on interlibrary loan that asks how long large libraries can continue to carry the load of requests from smaller libraries without some compensating return. In 1899 the Princeton University librarians proposed the formation of a "lending library for libraries" — an idea which has been realized in Great Britain but not yet in America. The National Union Catalog was established in 1900; and in 1927 that landmark among cooperative bibliographic works, the *Union List of Serials in Libraries of the United States and Canada* was published.

An example of an early proposal for cooperative collection development was unearthed by Berkeley's University Archivist recently. He found some 1899 correspondence from the aforementioned

Joseph Rowell to Herbert C. Nash, Stanford's first librarian, proposing a Berkeley/Stanford cooperative collecting plan. It could have served as a model for the successful grant proposal which the two universities submitted to the Sloan and Mellon Foundations some 80 years later. But generally, the concept of cooperative collection development came somewhat later than those of cooperative bibliography or interlibrary lending. One of the earliest cooperative collecting agreements Weber mentions is a 1931 formal agreement signed between Duke University and the Universtiy of North Carolina. This treaty is significant, not only for its pioneering example, but also for its long life; the Duke/North Carolina consortium is still alive, well, and garnering grants.

With all of this evidence that the resource sharing movement is an old one, it is fair to say that the greatly intensified thrust for resource sharing began in the forties. That decade saw the opening of the New England Depository Library, a model for cooperative space utilization, in 1942; and, in 1948, the birth of two major cooperative ventures, the Universal Serial and Book Exchange (USBE), and the Farmington Plan. All three of these 1940's innovations reveal a growing concern for quality and maintenance of collections. The succeeding three decades (the fifties, sixties, and seventies) produced a spate of resource sharing programs and of library networks and consortia to administer them. For example, the Midwest Interlibrary Center, later to become the Center for Research Libraries (CRL), opened in 1951; OCLC was incorporated in 1967; and the Research Libraries Group (RLG) was established in 1974, and expanded to RLG-2 in 1978.

It is unnecessary to belabor the history of the cooperative movement further. This brief summary demonstrates the persistance of librarians' belief that resources — whether of labor, space or collections — should be shared. Long before Daniel Gore and friends bade "Farewell to Alexandria" in their 1976 publication of that title,[5] librarians had recognized that knowledge is infinite, recorded knowledge just this side of infinity, and each library is a very finite place. True, for a brief while in the fifties and early sixties, we may have lost sight of this inevitable series of proportions. That was the period when America was pouring money into academic plant expansion, and librarians riding the growth wave launched some "vacuum cleaner" acquisitions programs ("Scoop up every scrap!"). But most of the time we really have known that no one library can possibly meet all the needs of its clients — that human curiosity and imagination will outstrip any collection of books. This is especially true in an era when the sheer volume of recorded information has, as we are fond of saying, exploded; and when the scholar/specialist has altered his work patterns, to function (quoting Lowell Martin again) "less in a limited spatial community and more in a far-flung interest community."⁶

Earlier I mentioned four categories of resource sharing: bibliographic access programs; information and bibliographic services; physical access programs; and cooperative collection development. Many resource sharing programs incorporate several or all of these elements. I would like to consider the impact on reference services of cooperative activities in each of these areas.

Bibliographic Access Programs

Let us begin with bibliographic access programs, since they are fundamental to the success of many other cooperative efforts. The goals which our profession has set and the projects on which we have embarked for the dispersal of bibliographic information can properly be called a bibliographic revolution. The reference librarian who looks today at the state of technological change and library catalogs may be inclined to echo Dickens' comment on another revolutionary time: "It was the best of times, it was the worst of times." The good aspects of the revolution are legion. Increasingly, we create our records through cooperatively-owned utilities which permit us to pool bibliographic information for reference purposes, as well as to eliminate duplicative processing. The computer-created records can be distributed to many locations in our own institutions and in others, freeing us from the rigid limitations of the single card file. The automated files promote the production of union catalogs, union lists of serials, and special bibliographies. The growing availability of online catalogs and databases enables us to outwit traditional limitations of bibliographic access and find the elusive conference, or the book the patron remembers only as "*Somebody* stopped at Eboli." (That is a real example of the familiar phenomenon I call the *partially*-known-item request. In case you've forgotten Carlo Levi's book about southern Italy, let me add that the "somebody" who stopped at Eboli is Christ. The question illustrates both the marvelous helpfulness of keyword search capability, and its inability to replace structured subject language.)

Yes, it is the best of bibliographic times, a period of exciting expansion of our power to identify and locate the intellectual record. But sometimes the period of transition is, for catalog users, the worst of times, too. Revolutions, even bibliographic ones, are messy. They are inevitably the enemy of order, until they have succeeded in establishing a new order. Many of us, when we look at our catalogs today, see in them the tension between the center and the widening gyre. We now create our bibliographic records for national and international shared use. They describe the entity, the work in hand, with what we trust is accuracy, and with a considerable degree of standardization. But when they are incorporated into our existing catalogs, which embody perhaps a hundred years of locally-developed idiosyncracies, they frequently fail to link the newly-cataloged books with related items in the collection. The technical process of shared cataloging is most cost-effective when records are accepted without emendation. Often an edition will be separated from its predecessor, an entry from its earlier form, or a series broken abruptly into separates if these ruptures will enable us to use a MARC, OCLC or RLIN record unaltered. Presumably we are gaining in processing efficiency, and hence in the number of volumes brought under bibliographic control; and that is a positive gain for reference service. However, we are losing some of the internal consistency of our catalogs, their capacity to relate like things. One striking example of this sacrifice of internal consistency to collective goals occurs to me. Before AACR-2 was adopted, many librarians had concluded that the new code was at best an extravagance, and at worst an irresponsible folly. (Richard DeGennaro said in the *Library Journal* last year, "AACR-2 promises to become cataloging's Full Employment Act.")[7] Nonetheless, dependence on Library of Congress cataloging and the use of cooperative utilities placed it beyond the power of most libraries even to consider rejecting the code, whatever problems its implementation poses for internal catalog consistency.

This is not a clarion call to reference librarians to oppose cooperative cataloging and renounce the Library of Congress with all its works and pomps. Obviously, the benefits of shared records are great; and the prospects for resolving the conflicts in our local catalogs are good, in the coming world of online files and authority systems. I will, however, use this forum to urge reference librarians to dedicate themselves to playing a major role in catalog development in the next decade. To do this, we need a sophisticated understanding of catalogs and how they work. We must know what online catalogs can do, and what kind of records they need to do it with. We must grasp the multiple functions of an interactive authority system, and what kinds of links are needed to restore and maintain the internal cohesiveness of our catalogs. And we must set up a mutual education program with our systems designers, working together to develop the online catalogs. Our direct user experience is an important element to bring to catalog planning. For example, the reference staff at Berkeley have now had experience with two online catalog systems which had no fixed-phrase search capability; that is, every search was treated by the computer as a keyword search, even when one could give it the exact title. I think a reference librarian on the design team could have argued that the capability for searching a known title quickly and directly is indispensable in a large catalog, no matter what other search capabilities the system has. (Incidentally, both systems have added or are adding fixed-phrase searching in their redesign phases.)

To sum up: cooperative efforts in bibliographic access contribute to the promise of a brave new catalog, flexible, distributed, responsible. They even make the prospect of putting our Humpty Dumpty together again — that is, of converting our old records to machine-readable form — look feasible. But the brave new catalog will meet our reference requirements, and those of our users, only if we learn to articulate those requirements with an understanding of their costs and benefits. (If you are inspired to begin a self-education program on the nature and function of the catalog, I might suggest a review of Cutter's *Rules*[8] as a starting point; followed, perhaps, by some of S. Michael Malonconico's thoughtful papers on the subject, for example his "Computers and Main Entry" in the *Wilson Library Bulletin*.)[9]

Information and Physical Access Programs

What about the impact of resource sharing on direct user services? As we said earlier, in creating our catalogs by means of cooperatively owned utilities, we create union catalogs; and the impact of this bibliographic phenomenon on reference, information and lending services is potentially limitless. As we reveal one library's holdings to the users of another, we create an inevitable demand for materials formerly unknown. The University of California nine-campus system is developing an online union catalog called MELVYL. It is at present only an experimental prototype catalog, with a very limited data base; but terminals are available for public "hands-on" use. In the year of its test operation interlibrary lending between UC libraries has gone up substantially, with the most dramatic lending increase (68.7 percent) at the library which happens to have the most records in the prototype catalog. The existence and availability of data bases like RLIN, OCLC and MELVYL, and the many computer output microform union lists like MULS (Minnesota Union List of Serials) and CALLS (California Academic Libraries List of Serials) have changed the essential nature of the reference response. We used to answer a lot of "Do you have?" questions with a simple negative. Now a "No" answer seems to call for a helpful corollary: "But Library X does." The improved literature search capabilities which result from online data bases and computer-produced block-buster bibliographic tools (such as the citation indexes) bring to light treasures which were formerly hidden. So the user's expectations are expanding too; if we don't volunteer the information about Library

X, he is very likely to ask, "Who does have it?" Increasingly our job is to locate information wherever it may be, and get it for the user quickly. The former simple "do you have?" question has become a complex reference question, requiring more staff time.

Fortunately (and by no means co-incidentally) cooperative information services and physical access services have expanded dramatically in recent years to meet this challenge of intensified user expectations. There is nothing very new about one library calling another for reference assistance; and there is certainly, as we have seen, nothing at all new about interlibrary lending. But the kind of structures we have created in recent decades to facilitate the exchange of information and books are in essence new, at least insofar as they transcend local political boundaries, and involve all types of libraries. I had the good fortune to be taught in library school by a great missionary of the public library movement, Carlton B. Joeckel. He was a quiet, low-keyed man, but he spoke with fervor of the challenges yet unmet of the library extension movement — the challenge we might call today the needs of the unserved. The many networks which cross type-of-library and political boundaries to make the richest resources widely available to all the people offer real promise of universal library and information service.

The National Center for Educational Statistics' *Directory of Library Networks and Cooperative Library Organizations, 1980*[10] lists 620 networks which are engaged, for mutual benefit, in cooperative activities broader than simple loan activities. They embody such services as distributed catalogs; central reference referral services (sometimes on a round-the-clock basis); computer search services; expedited loan and copy service; cooperative acquisitions; and continuing education programs for staff. Among the best known we might mention New York's METRO system, which incorporates all of the afore-mentioned activities; and the Illinois State network which, among other features, makes the collections of the University of Illinois accessible to readers throughout the state by means of the University Library's widely-distributed online catalog. But all of us can think of examples closer to home. And probably all of us have experienced some of the tensions these expanded services create for staffing and service priorities within the participating libraries. The problems of the net lender are, as we have seen, so old as to have been expressed in the literature of 1913. With the introduction of OCLC, and especially with the implementation of its interlibrary loan subsystem in 1979, the burdens of lending are being spread much more widely. As their holdings become visible in the data base, many small libraries are becoming net lenders, without much noticeable reduction of the large libraries' lending activities. At Berkeley we have experienced another change in lending patterns which may not be peculiar to us. With expedited delivery services between neighboring libraries, we are borrowing books we own. It's quicker to borrow a book from Stanford or UC Davis than to recall it from a Berkeley borrower. Out of all this I have distilled a truth which I am calling Polonius' Law: Interlibrary borrowing and lending will increase to exhaust the staff available. Then response time slows down, more resources are poured into interlibrary lending activities, collections in some areas get excessive use or abuse — and again the center shakes, and the threat of mere anarchy confronts us.

The principle of local, regional and national networks to provide information services to all is full of exciting promise. The actuality that is emerging combines with the blessings some problems of competing goods for the individual library. The prospect for resolution of these problems rests largely with the network structures themselves. These organizations can, if they will, deal with the key problem of inequity in partnerships. They can work out the *quid pro quo* for each partner that is essential for the survival of cooperative programs. By exchange of services, or by contract payments for service, or by strong lobbying for support of programs, the networks and consortia can structure a widening orbit of access to information, without imperiling the "centre" that is each member library.

Cooperative Collection Development Programs

Bibliographic access, physical access, information services — all these revolve around the great heart of our enterprise, the collections. Some of our most ambitious hopes for cooperation concern the coordination and rationalization of collection development, locally, regionally and nationally. We are impelled to cooperation in this area by a desire to extend the resources available to our own users, and by a readiness to make our riches available to that wider population serviced by the various networks. But equal to these motives, and sometimes outweighing them, is our awareness of the inexorable limits of space and budget. We have outgrown our stack space, and building funds are not forthcoming. We have watched book prices escalate faster than budget increases, and we have seen serials costs begin to devour monograph budgets. We see the universe of purchasable resources expand: personal papers and archives that formerly justified a scholar's trip to Washington in cherry blossom time can now be added to our own microform collections — for a price. Currently a small publisher is offering the entire Tibetan Buddhist canon for $15,000. The scholar who would formerly have been reconciled to the need to track it down in certain rare books collections will now have expectations of finding it locally. When rarities become in-print publications we are faced with difficult decisions. Which must we buy? Which might we borrow? How do we assure that *some* library will have them for loan? Efforts in the area of collection development cannot yet be considered the most successful cooperative programs; but they may be the ones which promise the most lasting benefits to users and to libraries in their attempts to create strong resources for scholarship and information.

Collection development programs can take several forms. One is a cooperative purchasing program for large research items. METRO has such a program to secure needed research materials within its region. The effort has been funded by contributions from member libraries, and a small federal grant. Probably the best-known American cooperative purchasing program is that of the Center for Research Libraries, which buys expensive microform sets at the membership's direction, drawing on funds provided from members' dues. (At present only about $25,000 per year is being devoted to this purpose.) The Center also collects in specified categories such as foreign dissertations and foreign newspapers, to free members from the obligation to acquire materials in these areas. A more substantial shared acquisitions effort is that of the nine University of California campus libraries and Stanford University. This program currently spends over half a million dollars annually in support of research materials needed in the region, but not needed on each campus. The funding for the program is skimmed off the top of the University's state book budget before book funds are allocated to the several campus libraries. Other such consortial cooperative acquisitions arrangements are emerging, and it seems to be an idea whose time has come.

But the really big question for rationalization of collecting, elimination of duplication, effective utilization of space, direct budgetary savings — the potentially big pay-off for cooperative acquisition, lies in the serials collection. The programs which will determine how the serials resources of America will be managed, how supported, how preserved are still in early evolutionary stages. The proposal for a National Periodicals Center which was presented in the Council on Library Resources' 1978 *National Periodicals Center Technical Development Plan*[11] did not find acceptance, for which I think there were some good reasons. The planners envisioned a central lending service modeled on the British Lending Library with a substantial collection — as many as 50,000 titles — of the most-demanded serials. They proposed reliance on existing research libraries for low-use serials. As a collection development and reference services librarian with a relentlessly client-focused view, I find that concept an inadequate prescription for America's serials problems. It seems to leave the major research libraries zealously preserving their low-use serials, presumably balancing their budgets by cancelling higher-use items, and then proceeding to borrow those items, at a considerable cost to all. The British system, admirable as it is, seems to me an unsuitable model for American planning. Great Britain is a small island, not much more than half the size of California. The British Lending Library's highly effective supermarket approach to journal access is complemented by the easily accessible scholarly resources of the British Library. (I suspect that scholars all over the Kingdom welcome an occasion to go to London for their research needs.) While the Yorkshire location of the British Lending Library may be deemed remote from centers of learning by British standards, it is to the American view conveniently situated in the midst of a comfortably-scaled region, a region of high population density and excellent transportation and communication facilities. An American plan for a national periodicals system must recognize that the wonders of telefacsimile transmission are not yet a practical reality. At present we deliver documents by mail, by parcel delivery service, or by our own bus systems; and these physical realities mean that for some time to come the most demanded works must be available close to the users.

In the absence of realistic national planning, some regional consortia are beginning to address the serials problem. In 1981 a group of eight southern university libraries, led by the University of Florida, was awarded a Title II-C grant for a serials project that involved both the creation of a shared data base and the rationalization of collections by assignment of responsibility and systematic cancellations. In the University of California/Stanford shared acquisitions program mentioned earlier, slow progress is being made toward the identification of important but low use serials to be supported by shared funds. The recognition is growing that unless we protect the nation's research reserves of serials, we are in danger of finding that important titles have disappeared in a rash of uncoordinated cancellations.

Reliance on another library's collections implies that we know what the other library has. The Florida-led consortium is creating a union serials list as an essential part of its project. The UC/Stanford group already enjoys the blessing of a very good union list of serials. But in some areas of our collections, and especially in that area which is for most of us the bottom of the iceberg, the great mass of older materials for which we do not have machine-readable records, the bibliographic access that makes for effective sharing is not yet on hand. The accurate knowledge that will be ours when we have completed retrospective conversion, put all the records in a linked OCLC/RLIN/etc. database, and developed local or national access systems that will permit our users to get at the Great Database readily — that precise knowledge is what we really want when we tell our users that we are relying on Library X. In the meantime, while we wait for Total Conversion, another very interesting cooperative collection development project promises substantial information about national collections. This is the collection conspectus project of the Research Libraries Group, an effort to analyze and compare member libraries' collections in defined subject areas. Each library identifies its collecting level for fairly specific segments of the L.C. classification scheme, using standard terminology to define collection levels. Languages collected or excluded, and other limitations are indicated. The results are displayed in a linear format which makes it possible to compare participants' collections in each subject. Conspectuses for language and literature, art and architecture, philosophy and religion, and East Asian language materials have been completed, and others are in process. Interest in the project is becoming widespread. Within the past year the Association for Research Libraries tested the conspectus as an instrument for analysis of its members' collections and decided to adopt it. There is work to do yet in refining the instrument for application in this larger setting, and libraries will undoubtedly have to choose their own time for participating in the laborious process; but the promised product should be a profile of America's scholarly resources that will be invaluable to reference and collection development librarians, and to users, in all kinds of libraries. I imagine the RLG/ARL conspectus sitting on the reference shelf right beside Lee Ash's *Subject Collections* (L.C. cataloging permitting). It will provide a broad picture of subject resources, to which Ash will serve as a detailed complement. With such a picture research libraries can re-examine their collecting policies, seeking areas where they can reduce expenditures with the assurance that their clients can still be served. Such cooperative collection agreements should enable us to expand the resources available within a reasonable time to our users.

Conclusion

We have seen that there is promise of problem-solving and service enrichment through a variety of cooperative programs. What can we do to insure that the promise is realized?

First, in embarking on a resource sharing program, it is important that a library consider the costs and benefits critically. We might begin by asking ourselves a few basic questions:

> What is the mission of our library?
> What is the goal of the resource sharing agreement?
> Will the projected agreement advance the mission of our library?

What is it going to cost us, directly and indirectly?
Is it worth it, to our library?

Those questions may sound too self-centered for the cooperative mode; but I am convinced that the resource sharing programs that thrive and prosper are based on enlightened self interest for all concerned. As one writer expressed it, an enduring resource sharing program will embody factors of profit and factors of equity for all members.[12]

Second, having decided that a cooperative program is desirable, librarians should be careful to advocate it with reason and realism. False advertising can raise misguided expectations, and lead to unwarranted disappointment on the part of governing bodies, funding authorities, or clients. I can think of two important areas where misunderstandings abound, and where librarians must improve their public relations if resource sharing efforts are to succeed.

One is the matter of the potential for dollar savings through resource sharing. The costs of cooperation are almost always immediate; the savings potential is frequently real, but long-term. DeGennaro states the case well in the article I quoted earlier:

> "Librarians have an urgent need to convince their local budget authorities, foundation officers, and corporate donors to provide the capital investment needed to complete the transition from manual to fully automated systems. We cannot bootstrap our libraries into the electronic age. For the last ten years librarians have been trying to build resource sharing consortia and the computer network systems to underpin them almost entirely from income derived from shared cataloging and other network service charges. They have made a good beginning, but income from these sources will not be enough to complete the job. Additional investment capital will be required if libraries are to make effective use of high technology."[13]

The other dangerous misunderstanding, dangerous at least to the research library, is the idea that by cooperative efforts we can maintain zero growth or steady-state libraries. This concept was advanced in the 1976 Atkinson Report[14] which mandated a fixed size for British university libraries; and it was the key issue at the 1975 Chicago conference of the Associated Colleges of the Midwest, "Touching Bottom in the Bottomless Pit. ACM Conference on Space, Growth and Performance Problems of Academic Libraries," from which emerged *Farewell to Alexandria*. It is essential that librarians understand and articulate the fact that, in the words of a

British librarian, "one cannot improve a research library by what amounts to a long-term replacement of its stock."[15] Knowledge is not outdated as quickly as it is produced.

In each of the areas discussed — bibliographic access, information and bibliographic services, physical access or delivery services, and cooperative collection development — there are potential benefits and inescapable costs for "the centre," the individual library and its patrons. The progress toward a universal bibliography of standard records is real and exciting; but meanwhile our catalogs-in-transition frustrate the user with mixed forms and split files. The development of consortia to facilitate exchange of information and of materials is impressive; but lending and borrowing are expensive, and the best document delivery service is still likely to be the bus your library runs to a neighboring library. The mapping of collections is proceeding, and will surely stimulate our awareness of what has been called "extended libraries" — resources beyond our walls; but "local sufficiency of stock," to quote Rothstein again, is still of prime importance to our patrons.

Therefore, we must plan our resource sharing programs carefully, realistically, and with one goal firmly in mind: increased benefits for our users. Lowell Martin has summed it up well:

> "Larger structures, greater territories, the far-flung interest group — but what about decentralization and local control? The individual local library on one side, the interlibrary cooperative structure on the other. As you build higher, do not neglect the foundation. Indeed, the purpose in the end is not a fancy superstructure but greater strength where resources and people meet."[16]

Let us bring all our public service knowledge to the challenge of assuring that for our patrons the center holds, things do not fall apart, and order, not anarchy, is loosed upon the world.

NOTES

1. Lines from "The Second Coming" are reprinted with permission of Macmillan Publishing Co., Inc. from *Collected Poems of William Butler Yeats*. Copyright 1942 by Macmillan Publishing Co., Inc., renewed 1952 by Bertha Georgie Yeats.

2. Nitecki, Danuta. "Requirements for a Systematic Review of Resource Sharing by Academic Libraries." Unpublished paper.

3. Weber, David. "A Century of Cooperative Programs among Academic Libraries." *College and Research Libraries*, May 1976. pp. 205–221.

4. Martin, Lowell A. "Emerging Trends in Interlibrary Cooperation." In *Cooperation between Types of Libraries: The Beginnings of a State Plan for Library Services in Illinois*, ed. by Cora E. Thomassen. Urbana, University of Illinois Graduate School of Library Science, 1969. (Atherton Park Institute No. 15)

5. Gore, Daniel, ed. *Farewell to Alexandria: Solutions to Space, Growth, and Performance Problems of Libraries.* Westport, CT, Greenwood Press, 1976.

6. Martin, op. cit., p. 7.

7. DeGennaro, Richard. "Libraries and Networks in Transition: Problems and Prospects for the 1980's." *Library Journal*, May 15, 1981. p. 1047.

8. Cutter, Charles A. *Rules for a Dictionary Catalog.* 4th ed., rewritten. Washington, DC, U.S. Government Printing Office, 1904; republished, London, The Library Association, 1953.

9. Malinconico, S. Michael. "Computers and Main Entry." *Wilson Library Bulletin*, September 1979.

10. Eckard, Helen. *Directory of Library Networks and Cooperative Library Organizations, 1980.* Washington, DC, National Center for Educational Statistics, 1980.

11. Council on Library Resources. *A National Periodicals Center: Technical Development Plan.* Washington, DC, The Council, 1978.

12. Rothstein, Samuel. "The Extended Library and the Dedicated Library: A Sceptical Outsider Looks at Union Catalogues and Bibliographic Networks." In, "The Future of the Union Catalogue; proceedings of the International Symposium on the Future of the Union Catalogue, University of Toronto, May 21–22, 1981." *Cataloguing and Classification Quarterly*, Vol. 2, Nos. 1/2, 1982.

13. DeGennaro, op. cit., p. 1048.

14. Great Britain. University Grants Committee. *Capital Provision for University Libraries: Report of a Working Party.* London, HMSO, 1976. (The Committee was chaired by Prof. R.J.C. Atkinson)

15. Higham, Norman. "The State of the Argument: United Kingdom." In, *Steady-State, Zero Growth and the Academic Library.* London, Clive Bingley, 1978. p. 40.

16. Martin, op. cit., p. 10.

The Impact of User Education and Computer Searching Programs on Reference Services

Kathleen Gunning

In the last decade, two program areas have come to occupy increasingly important places in the public services programs offered by academic libraries. These programs are bibliographic instruction and computer searching. The introduction and growth of these programs have led to an array of changes in the administration and implementation of library services. These programs are also important elements in the debate over the view of the reference librarian in academic libraries and in the proliferation of alternative career possibilities.

This paper will address the impact of bibliographic instruction and computer searching programs in the following areas: 1) organizational structure of public services divisions in academic libraries, 2) training needs of reference and other public service departments, 3) recruitment and evaluation criteria, 4) types of services offered at the reference desk, 5) methods of handling multiple responsibilities, 6) the image of the reference librarian inside and outside of academic libraries.

Organizational Structure

Libraries have used a variety of methods to administer and staff these programs. They may often be assigned to the reference department. In that case, participation in these activities can be included in each reference librarian's responsibilities, or the participation can be limited to a subset of librarians. Each method has its advantages. If all librarians in the department participate then the program can usually be carried on at a higher rate of activity and it is less vulnerable to disruption due to staff turnover. However, not all members of the department may be as equally well skilled at either bibliographic instruction or computer searching as they are at reference desk service. In addition, initial training followed by regular participation in these areas is important to achieve and maintain a high level of performance.

These two factors, unequal aptitudes of current staff and the need for special training and regular participation, have led many libraries to select only a few staff members for participation, especially on an initial basis. In some institutions this division of labor has been achieved by assigning different sets of responsibilities among reference staff. The specialization can lead to higher overall levels of interest in the program among the participating librarians, and it alleviates problems of training and of maintaining skills through regular participation. However, it also can leave the program more subject to interruption as a result of staff changes. In addition, those who participate in the program need to provide continuing information to other reference staff regarding current scope of the program, policies which govern faculty and student participation in the service, any fee structures, and so forth. This communication is necessary so that other staff may provide accurate information to library users at the reference desk.

Thus far, three possible organizational structures for handling these programs have been mentioned: first, including all reference librarians in these programs; second, within one department, selecting some librarians for one or both of these programs; third, creating separate departments of librarians who specialize mainly or entirely in one of those programs. A fourth possibility has emerged which appears to be gaining popularity, based on the increased number of position advertisements which are appearing in such publications as the *LJ Hotline* and the *Chronicle of Higher Education.* This alternative is the creation of a program coordinator position reporting either to the Head of Reference or Head of Public Services. This position frequently does not include supervisory responsibilities except for support staff, but does include responsibilities from program planning, staff training, public relations, and program evaluation.

This organizational structure has become useful in organizations which are committing fairly extensive resources in personnel and equipment to a program. It can be used whether participation in the program being coordinated is limited to a subset of the librarians in the department, includes all the librarians in the department, or includes librarians from outside of the department in which the coordinator is located. Another reason for the increasing popularity of coordinator positions, in addition to the staffing flexibility they offer, is the increasing administrative complexity of the position of the department head when the department is responsible for multiple service programs in which librarians both within and outside of the department may be involved to varying levels.

Obviously the number of the staff in the department will influence the need for a coordinator position. Small departments may operate multiple programs successfully without necessarily requiring the creation of a coordinator position or of a program committee for a user education or a computer searching program. However, as the activity level increases for either of these programs the department head will often desire the assistance which a coordinator position can provide.

Training Needs and Competencies Required for Bibliographic Instrucion and Computer Searching Services

The increased complexity of administering a staff which is involved in multiple service programs is paralleled by the increasingly diverse number of skills required of the staff who carry out these programs. Library user education and data base searching each require a set of special competencies in addition to the skills required at the reference desk. For example, someone who can interact well with individual users at a reference desk may not know how to present a lecture to a class.

In addition, the skills and knowledge needed to be an effective data base searcher are not identical to those needed by an instruction librarian. Therefore, when one or two of these sets of position responsibilities are added to the duties of current staff, this increased level of required skill should be considered. It will be useful to outline some of the competencies and personal attributes which are needed for high quality performance in each of these programs.

A computer searcher needs 1) a knowledge of the command languages of the various sytems used such as SDC, BRS, and Lockheed, 2) a knowledge of the organization and syndetic structure of the particular data bases to be searched, 3) typing skills, and 4) analytical abilities necessary for using Boolean logic combined with strong vocabulary skills. Some researchers have begun studies to identify common characteristics of proficient searchers, including deductive ability, analytical cognitive style, and facility with language.[1] Obviously these latter characteristics are also very helpful at the reference desk; however, in selecting reference desk staff, typically less attention is paid to analytical abilities than to good interpersonal skills, general subject knowledge, and understanding of reference tools and service policies.

An instruction librarian needs 1) the ability to organize a coherent and interesting presentation; 2) knowledge of techniques to enhance a presentation such as the use of audio-visual materials; 3) editing skills for the production of user guides, workbooks, and other written materials; and 4) the ability to interact well with groups of students in a teaching situation. Other skills could be identified as desirable ones for instruction librarians or for computer searchers; however, the basic issue is that the two lists of skills mentioned above are not directly required at the reference desk although they do enhance a person's ability to provide reference service. In addition the two lists differ from each other. Therefore the addition of one or both these responsibilities to a reference librarian position increases the complexity of the position and the number of skills which the person in the position must possess.

To carry out either or both of these programs successfully the organizers of the programs must make a commitment to the training of public services staff. This process should include the writing of a program statement with 1) goals for the bibliographic instruction or computer searching program, 2) some preliminary definition of required performance standards, and 3) the training required for staff to achieve those standards. On this basis it is possible to design appropriate training methods.

For example, if good writing and editing skills are needed to prepare a series of library guides, then a standard format can be designed. The staff can then be instructed in the use of this format and can prepare drafts of user guides following those directions. The drafts would then be reviewed and returned to the authors with comments. After preparing one or two guides according to this method there should be a common understanding as to the appropriate length of the guide, the level of sophistication in presentation appropriate for the target audience, the structure of presentation of the material in the guide, and so forth.

If the organizer of the data base searching program wishes to see that the staff have achieved a certain desired level of proficiency before those staff perform actual searches for library users, then sample search questions can be constructed. The staff members would then design search strategies for each of those questions. Their strategies would be reviewed by the trainer and compared with the strategies which the trainer had constructed. The staff members could work through sets of questions until their skills reached an acceptable level.

It is clear that such training programs involve a great deal of time and effort. The commitment of resources required is probably the principal reason that so few libraries provide adequate training for their staffs in either of these areas. However, there are substantial benefits to be derived from carefully constructed training programs. They will increase both the confidence and the ability of staff in carrying out the service program. Goal statements and training programs help to focus the program activities so that staff efforts can be concentrated and greater recognizable results can be obtained. At regular intervals, usually on an annual basis, the program should be evaluated. The staff members should receive recognition for their accomplishments in these areas and then new annual goals should be set for the program.

Once the initial training has been completed, continued regular participation in either program is important to maintain and further improve the levels of performance. This factor is especially crucial in data base searching because a detailed familiarity with system commands and indexing structures is needed for efficient use of the system. The efficiency requirement becomes obvious to both program administrators and library users when on-line time is charged by the minute and the cost is often totally or partially passed on to the users.

For any new service program there are advantages to beginning on a small scale and expanding the service gradually. It may be advisable to select a few librarians with particular interest in the program, train them carefully, set specific goals, and provide them with the resources in supplies and equipment that they need. Under these conditions the probability that they will achieve the goals is very high. The success of these staff in attaining the program goals will contribute to their sense of achievement. The recognition given to these staff may also encourage the participation of other staff who have previously hesitated to become involved.

Recruitment and Evaluation of Reference Librarians

It was mentioned that skills are needed to achieve proficiency in library instruction and in data base searching that are additional to the competencies needed in reference desk service. Some of these skills can be provided to staff through training. However, a reference librarian who can perform satisfactorily in providing traditional reference service may either be disinclined to participate in the new programs even when urged to do so, or may lack certain analytical or teaching skills needed for success.

As a result, the introduction of either a data base searching program or a bibliographic instruction program will influence the criteria used to evaluate staff who participate in the program. This change in criteria will usually occur gradually as the participants and the program administrators become increasingly familiar with the performance levels and skills needed. Staff who engage in both library instruction and computer searching programs as well as reference desk service will eventually be required to satisfy considerably more rigorous criteria than librarians who engage only in reference desk service. It is hard for some to perform well in all three areas.

One problem which occurs with some frequency involves reference staff already employed by the library who do not wish to fulfill these new program responsibilities or are unable to do so well. The program administrator must then decide whether to require the participation of these staff who were not originally hired to perform such functions. This problem becomes particularly acute when the library has a reference/bibliographer structure. In this situation each reference librarian is responsible for providing collection development, library instruction and computer searching in assigned subject areas as well as staffing a reference desk. Faculty and students learn to identify one person as the primary supplier of their library service needs. The information and experience derived from each of the service programs enhances the librarian's ability to meet user needs in the other service areas.

The success of this structure hinges upon the ability of each reference librarian to perform competently in each of these areas. Librarians on the staff should gradually receive training in each area and attempts should be made to diagnose and overcome any deficiencies in performance. However, it may eventually become apparent that, for example, a person continues to feel extremely uncomfortable when teaching a class of students and therefore does it poorly. At that time the administrator of the library instruction program may well decide that it is not in the best interests of the program or of the individual to require the person's participation in that activity. If the person has strengths in another service area he or she may be assigned more work for that service and relieved of responsibility in the problem area.

In addition to changing the criteria for assessing the performance of librarians on the staff, library instruction and computer searching programs have led to alterations in the qualifications sought in recruiting reference librarians. It is more and more frequently expected that applicants will have either coursework or work experience in both of these program areas. Some institutions request applicants to send samples of instruction materials that they have prepared or to do a sample presentation. Applicants may be asked which data bases they have searched, how many searches they have performed, and the approximate average length of time of their searches.

Library school students who desire a career in reference services should be made aware of these developments and seek the necessary coursework to meet these requirements. Librarians working in public services who have not already been engaged in computer searching or bibliographic instruction would be advised to gain this experience both to enhance the services they can provide in their present position and to improve their prospects when they begin to apply for other positions.

Services Offered at the Reference Desk

Bibliographic instruction and computer searching services have changed the organizational structures, training needs and evaluation and recruitment criteria for reference departments. They are also causing alterations in the philosophy and forms of service being provided at the reference desk. The traditional pattern of reference service in academic libraries consists of staff stationed at a desk waiting to be approached by users with questions. When a question is asked, the reference librarian directs the user to materials which will answer the question, or if time permits, finds the answer for the user in available print or microform sources.

During the last few years many libraries have placed the terminals of bibliographic utilities such as OCLC and RLIN at reference desks. While these data bases were not originally intended for public services use, they have been a great boon to reference librarians. Positive experiences with these data bases, and the rapidly increasing popularity of regular computer searching services, have inspired some librarians to incorporate the use of data bases maintained by Lockheed, SDC, BRS and other commercial vendors in ready reference services. These data bases are being accessed to provide information which is not yet indexed in printed sources, or which could only be obtained through a time-consuming search through many printed sources. The sophisticated subject access provided by online data bases can enable librarians to answer questions rapidly which they previously might not have been able to answer at all.

Policies for the use of online data bases in reference desk service need to be written carefully in order to distinguish those brief searches for specific information from the more extensive searching done away from the reference desk in which extensive bibliographies can be compiled or exhaustive searches carried out. This distinction is necessary because of the time constraints imposed on the staff at a busy reference desk.

The influence of user education programs is being manifested in several ways. At some libraries the pattern of having staff wait at the desk for questions is being changed. Reference staff are scheduled as "floaters" to make rounds of the card catalog and reference collection areas. They are expected to carry out an active policy of reference service in which the library staff take the initiative in approaching patrons who may need assistance rather than waiting to be asked.

Projects such as term-paper clinics combine reference desk service and library instruction. Well-taught library-use classes tend to generate questions for the reference desk staff because users are more aware that an extensive variety of reference tools exists and they seek the sources that will satisfy their information needs.

These examples illustrate the impact of computer searching and bibliographic instruction programs on reference desk services thus far. It seems likely that in the future the proliferation of online catalogs and the consequent decentralization of access to information regarding library collections, as well as new advances in data base creation will further transform reference services.[2]

Methods of Coping with New Service Configurations

The changes in organizational structures in sets of position responsibilities, in training, evaluation, and recruitment criteria, and in traditional patterns of reference desk service are placing rigorous demands on all staff involved in these programs. An increasingly extensive and complex set of skills is now required of public service librarians. The peak use periods of the various service programs sometimes coincide so that the staff must function at a very high level of efficiency and flexibility in order to respond promptly to the different service needs. While this intensity of user demand and the opportunity for librarians to engage in many different activities is challenging and highly satisfying, it can also be exhausting. Recent articles by Neville[3] and by Ferriero and Powers[4] note that job stress and burnout are occupational hazards for library staff involved in direct service to the library user. These pressures can be intensified when librarians must satisfy many competing demands for different types of service.

Administrators and staff involved in these programs need to develop mechanisms to deal with stress. One important method is the establishment of priorities among the various programs within any given time period, and of implementation schedules for achieving service goals. This technique enables staff to make rational and consistent choices among multiple requests. It also allows the group to review its progress in meeting its service goals.

Another method is the fostering of mutual support systems among the staff. These support systems would include, 1) frequent effectively run meetings to review goals, plans and activities; 2) prompt recognition of staff achievements; 3) regular consultations among staff and program administrators so that small problems can be solved rapidly before they become major irritations; 4) short periods of quiet time between periods of hectic contact with library users. The use of these techniques can assist staff in reducing the stress to manageable levels.

Two additional changes resulting from these programs are a shift in the perceptions of librarians and library services by users and the evaluation of alternative careers for librarians as information brokers.

User perceptions of library services tend to be enhanced when librarians perform computer searches for them.[5] The savings in time and the improved subject access which are offered by computer search services can enable library users to see the library as an important information center. An effective library instruction program can present librarians as approachable, knowledgeable, and helpful people rather than as the custodians of library books.[6]

The mastery of the skills needed for proficiency in these programs has also prompted some librarians to reevaluate their own activities. A number of librarians have chosen to market these skills to the public on a freelance basis rather than offering them as an employee of a library. Those librarians have moved a long way from the traditional image of the reference librarian while still participating in the delivery of information services.

Conclusion

The emergence and proliferation of library instruction and computer searching programs have had several important consequences for reference departments. They have led to more complex organizational structures in order to manage these programs. They require considerable additional training for reference staffs. More rigorous criteria are being used to evaluate and recruit reference librarians. Traditional reference desk service has adopted various aspects of these programs. Reference librarian positions have become more challenging, more interesting, and more stressful. Library administrators need to provide methods which will enable their staffs to cope with those stresses. The image of the reference librarian is changing both in the eyes of library users and in the eyes of reference librarians themselves.

These many developments are changing the outlooks and activities of reference staffs in a very productive and stimulating fashion. Administrators of these programs need to continue working on the problems of workloads, training, assignment of position responsibilities, and stress which are hampering the ability of reference librarians to provide the high quality reference and related information services which they wish to offer. The various information service programs should be integrated as fully as possible into one total system of services. This integrated service model offers one of our best chances to define the academic library as an active information-provider and a recognized participant in the university's research enterprise.

NOTES

1. Donna R. Dolan and Michael C. Kremin, "The Quality Control of Search Analysts," *Online* 3 (April 1979).

2. Pat Ensor, "The Expanding Use of Computers in Reference Service," *RQ* 21 (Summer 1982).

3. Sandra H. Neville, "Job Stress and Burnout: Occupational Hazards for Service Staff," *College and Research Libraries* 42 (May 1981).

4. David S. Ferriero and Kathleen A. Powers, "Burnout at the Reference Desk," *RQ* 21 (Spring 1982).

5. Richard Dreifuss, "Library Instruction in the Database Searching Context," *RQ* 21 (Spring 1982).

6. Thomas Kirk, "Course-Related Library Instruction in the 70's," in Hannelore B. Rader, ed., *Library Instruction in the Seventies: A State of the Art* (Ann Arbor: Pierian Press, 1977).

Evaluation and Measurement of Reference Service:
Problems, Approaches, and Potential

Maurice P. Marchant

My assignment is to discuss evaluation of reference service. I would like to begin with a general discussion of evaluation and measurement and then apply them to reference service.

Evaluation is best discussed in its broader contexts as parts of systems and planning theories. Both call for some system of feedback or monitoring by which data are gathered for evaluation, allowing readjustment as required to maintain the system's viability. To assure an adequate understanding of what I am talking about, let me describe briefly both theories.

Systems Theory

Systems theory is concerned with the processing of inputs into outputs. A system might be very simple or it might be highly complicated. Reference service systems are never simple. Indeed, the more we study them the more complex they appear. Inputs include, but are not limited to, reference queries, reference personnel, the reference collection, housing and furnishings including the telephone and, today, terminals connecting the reference department to OCLC, RLIN, and other networking systems. Processes include question negotiation, search techniques, and interlibrary loan procedures among others. Outputs include the resultant service, of whatever quality or character. Libraries have traditionally had great difficulty measuring output, and this difficulty has retarded our ability to improve our performance.

Again, systems theory is concerned with the processing of inputs into outputs, so the nature of reference service is determined by the character of inputs and processes found in the reference service. Personnel ignorant of the content of basic reference tools and inept at interpersonnel communication are not likely to provide quality service. Systems theory also carries a second important concept: namely, a change in one part of the system is likely to affect other parts. For example, reducing the reference staff is likely to force those remaining to modify the communication processes or search strategies they use, thus reducing the quality of their service. Even when inputs remain constant, one process modification is likely to affect other processes, even in unintended ways.

General systems theory can be divided into open and closed systems. Libraries, and library reference service, are open systems. They are open in that they are not self-sufficient, requiring input from their environment and exporting a product or output. Two generalities from open system theory are important: (1) outputs are exchanged in the environment for renewed input, and (2) the value of the output is determined in the environment, not by the system. If this theory is correct, and I believe it is, librarians have much to learn from its application. Its implications are profound and, while too extensive to be dealt with in detail here, some ought to be observed. First, note that it is concerned with tracing the cycling of energy through the system, into the environment, and back into the system. The amount of energy can grow or diminish depending on the ratio between the cost of processing a unit of output and the value the environment places on that unit and is willing to trade for it. If a library expends more resources on its service than its community is willing to pay for it, the library, as a system, will run down. To assure against that happening, the library must be sensitive to its community's value system and accommodate to it. In order to accommodate, it needs feedback that reports how various components of the system are performing and how the environment is reacting to the system, especially its products.[1]

Feedback provides the data for the evaluation used in making the operational adjustments necessary for system viability and wellbeing. One's perception of the system, its component parts and their interactions, must conform to reality if the evaluation is to be used successfully in improving the system's stability and performance. So must the evaluator properly perceive the salient environmental influences. Furthermore, since these influences are in continuing flux, their changing patterns must be recognized. Profit-making organizations learn to react to their environment largely through an economic model. A car dealer learns to offer the type of automobiles that the public is interested in buying. His cars do not have to appeal to everyone, or even a majority of the people, just as long as he has enough active customers to keep his business at a healthy level. Those who use his service contribute a direct input to his company. Non-profit organizations operate differently. For example, the legislature, acting on the governor's budget proposal, sets a public university's annual budget. Following hearings with deans and directors, the president and his administrative aides divide up the available funds and set the university's — and library's — budget. But the primary library users, students and faculty, have little direct influence. However, their indirect effect may be very compelling, and we need to learn how to exploit such potential sources of influence to our own best advantage. Influence structures exist even in systems that operate more by political than economic models. The better we understand their structure, the greater will be our ability to affect them and to adjust to them as they change.

Open systems can improve their stability largely in three ways. They can reduce the per unit cost of output production, they can modify the output so that it is more valuable, and they can modify the environment's perception of the current product so that it is perceived as more valuable within the power structure that approves the input. But in planning a modification, the system would be well advised to assure an adequate monitoring system by which it will acquire feedback needed for evaluation and, as needed, readjustment.

Planning Theory

Planning is a process which people design to achieve the ends they deem desirable. It starts with goal-setting. Please note that it is not merely projecting the future. Rather, it is intended to mold the future, to affect future conditions in desirable ways. While all planning carries the risk of failure, some planning characteristics can be built in to reduce the probability of failure. Planning is more likely to succeed under the following circumstances. (1) Goals are realistic, specific, and their accomplishments observable and measureable. (2) The magnitude of required change from the current to the desired situation has been established. That is, the need for change has been well assessed. (3) The process by which the change is to be made has been chosen only after serious consideration of several alternatives, and those who must operate it have been involved in evaluating the possibilities and choosing from among them. (4) Before putting it into operation, a monitoring system has been designed by which data can be drawn for later evaluation. Often appropriate for such an evaluation would be data regarding the situation prior to the change. Those data should be available from a good needs assessment, and it should provide a baseline for considering the success of the plan as it goes into operation. Obviously, relevant and accurate measurements enhance the evaluation and readjustment processes. (5) Reviews are regularly scheduled during which the feedback data are interpreted and used for readjusting the plan for continued, improved operation. Commonly, improvements in the plan's success are made by adjusting either goals or processes. A third category of change that deserves consideration is to improve the monitoring system.[2]

Measurement

I would like now to turn to the concept of measurement, which is critical in evaluation. Measurement includes everything done to arrive at a numerical estimate. It includes the measuring instrument, its use, the skill of its user, and sometimes other factors. Obviously, error in measurement retards the quality of evaluation possible. That is not to say that absolute accuracy is required. Error can be tolerated within bounds. Two terms that deserve particular attention are precision and accuracy. Measuring my weight at 182.148 pounds would be very precise, well beyond the capacity of the scales I use, though at one brief moment it may have been correct. Estimating it between 160 and 200 pounds is a statement of accuracy, or perhaps inaccuracy.

One may predict a value for one variable from readings of other related variables. For example, height and weight might be related, allowing the prediction of weight by a formula using height as a predictor, but recognizing a potential error. Suppose I had an equation that predicted my weight at 175.486 pounds with a standard error of estimate of 10.5. I would know that about two-thirds of the people my height weigh between 165 and 186 pounds and that, given the error estimate, the prediction ought to be rounded off. The precision is very high and a little silly given the lack of accuracy.

Sampling Error

Measurement estimates often result from sampling. If a phenomenon occurs many times, attempting to measure every instance in order to get an average and a range of differences may not be feasible. Sampling often is more realistic, but it allows two types of error to creep in: noise and bias. A good sample is a partial selection, drawn from a larger population, that accurately represents the values and diversity of the population. Under those conditions, a study of the sample will provide the same measurements as one would get by measuring every instance of the population. We resort to sampling because the entire population may not be available for study or to save energy and time. Lacking population data, one is never completely sure of the extent to which the measurements drawn from a sample contain noise and bias.

Sometimes measurement error is systematic and sometimes it is random. Systematic error biases the final measure while random error, which we call noise, widens the range around the estimate but doesn't bias it. Let me give some examples. Suppose your administrator requires you to mark down the number of reference contacts you experience each day, dividing them into directional, ready reference, and extensive search categories. If the staff size on a reference desk is determined by the number of extensive searches carried out, you might be inclined to inflate that count, thus biasing the results. With directional questions, you might forget to mark some down as you work, so at the end of the day you try to make up for it. In this hypothetical situation, you try to be accurate, but sometimes you mark too many and sometimes too few. They average out, however, so that the only errors are in the distributions. This type of error is called noise. It spreads the distribution of daily contacts but does not misrepresent the daily average.

Reliability and Validity

Noise and bias affect reliability and validity, two valuable characteristics of evaluative measurements.

Reliability is characterized by consistent, trustworthy measurements. Noise, or random error, reduces reliability. Even though the average of the sample reading might be reasonably accurate, the random error will result in a wider standard deviation than is deserved and, therefore, lowered accuracy and lowered confidence in the results than the true measurements would have provided. A reliable instrument will give the same reading under the same circumstances each time it is used. It may or may not be wrong, but it will be consistent.

Validity is an attribute of measuring what is intended. Much research is carried out using instruments of questionable validity. Let me give two examples from library education. Commonly, undergraduate grade point averages are used to predict the likely success of students applying for admission to library school, with a 3.0 GPA as the minimum for full degree status. Exceptions are sometimes allowed for some students below that point to be admitted provisionally. Every commencement, in April and August, we give an award to the graduating student who has demonstrated the greatest professional improvement. Most of the time, the award goes to a student accepted provisionally and who, had we adhered strictly to the standard, would not have been admitted but who fully justified our exception by performing outstandingly. Similar, we do not find a high relationship between academic performance intended as professional preparation and later performance on the job. Some people who are outstanding students do poorly as practitioners; and then, alas, occasionally they return to the university as teachers of the same misperceptions that led to their poor performance. So the use of the GPA as the sole instrument for selecting either students or staff is a good deal less valid than most of us want.

Validity, like reliability, is a matter of degree. Like reliability, it is affected by noise. Unlike it, validity is also reduced by bias, that is, systematic error. High validity requires keeping both random and systematic error low. A common threat to validity is combining several measures into one. For example, combining all types of reference contacts in a single enumeration would cause difficulties in their interpretation. Thus, classifying them into several types would enhance the validity of their measurements.

Some people would say that, given the innate humanness of reference service, attempts at measuring its component parts are futile and inappropriate. Poor measurements indeed can be harmful. On the other hand, to declare that something is innately not measurable is to deny human ingenuity. We continue to improve our ability to measure not only quantitative aspects but qualitative as well. Is that important? Indeed it is. The ability to measure enhances understanding. The more precise the measurement, the more specific the comprehension. Some scholars even claim that the inability to measure results is the inability to understand.[3]

Reference Service Evaluation

Having discussed the basics of evaluation and measurement, the time finally arrives for discussing the evaluation of reference service. Unfortunately, while reference service has experienced much development, its evaluation has not. Much hard work is required before reference service can be measured reliably and validly. That failure has been a prime retardant of the development of good causal models of reference service. It also inhibits reference staffs and administrators from making local adjustments that would improve reference service.

Reference service evaluations can be divided into two categories: quantitative and qualitative.[4]

Quantitative measures commonly consist of enumerating requests for service in such categories as directional, ready reference, extended service, and reader's advisement. The value of such measurements is limited to telling how much service is requested. It does not report how much is provided nor the quality of the service. Its primary use is to demonstrate change in user expectations and for setting staffing patterns and levels.

While it has the asset of subdividing service into several categories, it contains several weaknesses. The categories lack distinctive definitions. As a consequence, assigning individual contacts to the categories is often arbitrary and inconsistent. Further, many librarians keep inaccurate records from lack of concern. Some may overstate contacts on purpose. Niether reliability nor validity can be confirmed, and both are suspect.

Measures of the quality of reference service are based on the extent to which the patron gets the information requested. Success can be measured by the reference librarian, the patron, or a disinterested expert observer. The measurement is often either a count of successful contacts or the ratio of successful to total contacts.

The best reference service research has used unobtrusive procedures wherein librarians are asked prestructured questions for which the correct answers were already known. Success is giving the same answer established by the expert. Success rates vary considerably from one library to another and average about 50 percent in both academic and public libraries. They contrast sharply with librarians' judgment that their responses are 95 percent correct. The differences may have resulted partly from the use in unobtrusive testing of questions that are harder than those asked by real patrons. But also contributing to the disparity is the librarian's failure to know that a wrong answer has been given. Furthermore, the questions not properly answered are often readily available. Let me give some examples. Of 40 academic reference librarians asked who the President of the American Library Association is, 11 did not give the right answer. Only three located the correct name of the ASIS president, and 60 percent did not find the zip code for Behrend College in Erie, Pennsylvania.[5] Knowing that such questions are not being properly answered in a given library ought to provide a point of departure for finding out why and rectifying at least some of the reasons.

What are the reasons? They come from many sources. For some questions, answers may not be available. Others may be so complicated or technical as to require a scholar specializing in a very narrow field to give a satisfactory explanation. But other failures are within the librarian's ability to control. Some reference librarians may not be adequately conversant with basic reference tools. Others may not keep up with the current news. A staff may be so overwhelmed with work it resorts to poor responses or refuses to answer some categories of question. Poor question negotiation may result in misunderstandings of what patrons want. Much of the failure might be overcome if libraries would simply set standards of expectation for reference service and commit the reference staff to meet those standards. Whatever the reason, identification and correction is unlikely without an evaluation process. If lack of knowledge is the culprit, educate your staff. If their skills are poor, train them. If they do not care, motivate or replace them.

One weakness in measuring reference service is our tendency to think of it as one generality rather than of its component parts. The generalization makes measurement difficult. Perhaps dividing it into more specific components would improve our ability to measure the parts. We might find that the various aspects differ in how we might best deal with them.

Conclusion

The demand for accountability regarding the use of resources made available for societal purposes has been growing in recent years and will continue to grow in the future. Society wants evidence that the resources it provides are accomplishing desirable goals. Evaluation and measurement are cognitive tools helpful in accomplishing that expectation. They also can help us improve our service so that we can be proud of our accounting. This presentation has been intended to convince you of the value of evaluation and to introduce some attributes of good measuring which you might find helpful.

As we improve the quality of evaluation of reference services, researchers will be able to develop causal models that will be applicable in many libraries. But the individual library need not wait for their design, for much can be done now. Libraries willing to invest some time, effort, imagination, and a little money will find that planning and evaluation provide the insight from which librarians can improve their performance and service. I think librarians realize the truth of that rationale.

Why, then, are libraries reluctant to plan and evaluate? Why, instead, do many librarians not set aside time for evaluation? The major excuse given is that they are so overburdened with work that they do not have time. Work is equated in their minds with operational tasks, and planning is something else. Moreover, they are sure, even without evidence, that whatever they are doing is justified. I would suggest some other reasons. First, they are comfortable doing what they do, and their evaluation and planning skills are not well developed. We must develop a different norm. To become comfortable in those activities, librarians need training and experience, and it is up to administrators to see that they are provided. Second, they are afraid of what an evaluation will uncover. Even if they are doing pretty well, they are likely to feel nervous and threatened, somewhat like the smoker who found the reports on the effects of smoking so nervewracking that he gave up reading. New information is often threatening, but administrators can design evaluation processes so as to emphasize the opportunities and rewards for improvement and recognition and minimize threat and fear.

Improved evaluation in libraries is largely in the hands of administrators. While they should involve their staff in the process, administrators are the critical element that will determine whether evaluation occurs. Whether it will improve service or not we can never be sure, for planning always involves a risk. Evaluation and planning will not assure improved service, but the lack of them will surely retard it.

NOTES

1. For an explanation of the open system theory of organizations, see Daniel Katz and Robert L. Kahn, *The Social Psychology of Organizations* (New York: Wiley, 1966), especially chapters 2 and 3. For an explanation of its application to libraries, see Maurice P. Marchant, *Participative Management in Academic Libraries* (Westport, CT: Greenwood Press, 1976), chapter 2.

2. A good general book on planning theory is Russell L. Ackoff, *A Concept of Corporate Planning* (New York: Wiley-Interscience, 1970). Duane Webster, *Planning Aids for the University Library Director*. University Library Management Studies Office Ocassional Papers no. 1 (Washington: Association of Research Libraries, 1971) is a good brief statement on library planning. More comprehensive and recent help is in Charles R. McClure, ed., *Planning for Library Services: A Guide to Utilizing Planning Methods for Library Management* (New York: Haworth Press, 1982).

3. Jeffrey Katzer, Kenneth H. Cook, and Wayne W. Crouch, *Evaluating Information: A Guide for Users of Social Science Research* (Reading, MA: Addison-Wesley, 1979), chapter 9, contains a good brief discussion on measurement.

4. For a reasonably good summary of research into evaluating reference service, see F.W. Lancaster, *The Measurement and Evaluation of Library Services* (Washington: Information Resources Press, 1977), chapter 3.

5. Marcia J. Myers, "The Accuracy of Telephone Reference Services in the Southeast: A Case for Quantitative Standards," in *Library Effectiveness: A State of the Art*, eds. Neal K. Kaske and William G. Jones (Chicago: Library Administration and Management Association, American Library Association, 1980), pp. 220–33.

"Fees or Free"

Anne K. Beaubien

Some people would claim that asking the head of a fee based service to discuss the pros and cons of charging for information is like inviting a professional baseball team to play the local high school: there is no doubt which "side" will win. I do not intend to defend my position, however, but merely to explain its history and rationale in the academic library setting. I should also mention at the outset that my business MITS (The Michigan Information Transfer Source) is run on a cost recovery basis and is not for profit. All the money received goes back to the library. MITS is an integral part of the University of Michigan Library System. And, as director of that service, I report to the Associate Director for Public Services. Every service needs a philosophy and there are several philosophical issues involved for academic libraries considering establishing fees for reference service.

Arguments against Fees

The first issue to examine is the argument for and against charging user fees in libraries. At the most basic level is the concept that information is free. A democracy is based on the philosophy of equal access to information — free information — to all citizens as a matter of right. Fees for information service restrict access to information to those who can afford the fees and thus deprive others of their right to access information. Therefore, the argument goes, existing tax supported libraries should not charge for library services — even specialized services like data base searching. Libraries have a long tradition of providing "free" service which is in fact not free but is supported indirectly by a specific group of people through tuition, taxes, (property and income), or through the budget of the parent organization, in our case the university or college. One of the most important points that I can make today is that we are *not* discussing the charging for information, but rather it is the *service* to gather the information for which we charge: the expertise to know where to look for information efficiently and effectively, the staff time necessary to retrieve the information, and the direct, calculable expenses incurred while doing so (photocopies, postage, long distance telephone, online time, etc.).

Another argument against library fees is that everyone shares in the benefits provided by libraries — no one is excluded from their use or benefit. In theory, using materials in the library does not deplete the supply on the shelf. And, once material is selected, purchased, and cataloged the cost of each additional use is zero (if you do not count binding or replacement pages). Therefore, the entire academic community should pay for library services through tuition and the general budget of the academic institution. This general philosophy provides for basic library services but doesnot address special programs or extraordinary services that are not needed by everyone. Necessary fees to cover all the basic *and* special services for everyone are potentially very high.

The last argument against fees suggests that if fees are levied we are making students and faculty pay twice — once with tuition and then again for direct charges for service. The answer to that argument is that it is a lot better for users to pay twice and get exactly what they need than to pay once and receive services not specific enough for their needs. In my view, when there are fees for special services the financial burden of having them available is borne by the individuals or companies who benefit.

Arguments for Fees

The arguments for charging fees have been alluded to somewhat. First, a strong case can be made for adopting users fees for certain, special services (especially those based on expensive new computer technology). In many cases the choice is charging for special services or not offering them at all. Secondly is the point made above that users who pay through tuition and for a special service get exactly what they need. General users should not have to support the high cost of special programs. Thirdly, if users pay twice, the money received may be used to reduce the amount of indirect "taxation" or to finance new or expanded information programs. Fourth, with library budgets being cut back charging fees for non-primary clientele is a way to keep the library's resources open to them and to justify providing services to them at all. Lastly, libraries have charged for services in the past for such things as replacing lost library cards and photocopying. Both libraries and users have accepted the idea that copying service should be paid for by the person who uses it.

Part of the discussion about charging fees in libraries is a matter of tradition. We are used to paying for expertise from a doctor or lawyer. Even though we can look up some medical information ourselves in *Physicians Desk Reference* or a medical text we usually choose to pay for the services of a physician to diagnose and interpret our problems. We are not used to paying the reference librarian for analyzing our research questions and suggesting search strategies and solutions.

Characteristics of Fees

When determining if users charges will be instituted there are several characteristics of fees and issues to examine (Kranich, 1980, p.1050). One should determine if the intent of the fee is to ration a service which is in limited supply or to reduce its frivolous use. For example, a fee for online time might be established so that people use it for questions related to coursework or research that could not have been answered just as effectively manually. Charges for interlibrary loan service could be instituted to limit the number of requests submitted by any one person or individual. The nature of the service is also an important characteristic. In some cases, use of a public service is too diffuse to identify its users. For example, the cost of library hours, a browsing collection, telephone reference, library display cases, and cataloging and classification of materials cannot be ascribed to one population group as the sole beneficiary.

The third characteristic related to fees is their administrability: it may cost more to collect a fee than the revenue generated. I find it amazing that there are libraries issuing invoices for amounts less than $1.00. I dare say that the billing procedures at all of our institutions exceeds $1.00. The possible mechanics of charging for quick reference all seem awkward to me but it is a theoretical possibility. Absurd possibilities include a stop watch to time and bill transactions, prepaid coupons, and a coin box/meter. A more graceful way to consider handling such billing would be to have prepaid contracts with various departments or companies to cover unlimited quick reference for the year or month. It may take some experimentation to arrive at the formula for the correct "flat fee." If there are user fees to get into the building, reference should negotiate with the administration for a "cut of the gate" to help support the inevitable reference activities of these patrons.

Equity is a fourth characteristics of user fees, and one can look either at classes of users or the nature of the information to which you are providing access. User charges may place a disproportional burden of cost on a class of individuals least capable of paying (i.e., students, or those most capable of paying, e.g., business and industry) so the ramifications of any fee schedule will have to be thought through. In addition to looking at classes of users, there is also the cost of the information to consider. If you charge for online computer time you will notice great differentials in cost from one data base to another. This makes the cost of doing research in a subject field like chemistry far more expensive than doing research in, say, education. So, the question becomes, is it fair to charge the person doing research in chemistry more than the person doing research in education?

A further complication, under the issue of equity, are those information sources which are only available for a fee. There are at least three different scenarios with data bases. Some files, like *Psychological Abstracts,* have only part of the data base printed in the hard copy. Since January 1980 references to dissertations, technical reports and chapters in books are available only in the online version. Some data bases, like CIS (Congressional Information System), have access points online that are not available in the printed form, like witness affiliation index and the free text subject capability in the abstracts. Then, there are data bases like **ABI/INFORM** which have no printed equivalent at all. In these cases the decision process for charging becomes less clear.

Availability is the final characteristic which influences charges. In the library itself, could the service be offered if charges were not levied? In the marketplace, are the services for which you would like to charge available locally? How will your price structure compare to theirs?

Private vs Publically Supported Institutions

Academic library patrons are members of institutions which have well defined goals. Thus, it is easy to determine who is served and for what purpose. A common mission statement for an academic library would be to "provide for the research, instruction, and informational needs of the university or college community." Primary clientele include faculty, students, and staff. Non-primary clientele include business, industry and individuals not associated with the institution.

There are some philosophical differences, I think, in how outside users are handled depending on whether you are a publicly funded or privately supported institution. In a state-supported institution, a portion of the taxes paid by businesses have been contributed to the library. There is some obligation then to having the stacks open to them if they should visit (assuming you have open stacks). Written requests would be put in the queue with other work but might be given a lower priority since companies do not qualify as primary clientele in the mission statement of the academic library. Providing a service free, but taking "forever" to do it, is a choice many libraries make because they have no obligation to give outside users an expedited service.

Private schools are in a strong position to restrict access to their collections and reference. Outsiders have no right to have access to the building, let alone borrow from the collection, or have a fast photocopy service. Any public funding in the form of research grants from such agencies as the National Endowment for the Humanities or the National Science Foundation, are for a specific project and provide little, if any, of the support to the library or institution as a whole. Since the bulk of the support for private schools comes from private sources they can administer their resources as they so choose.

I would like to discuss several different aspects of reference for which one could consider charging a fee together with some of the changing environmental factors which have affected these services in recent years. The topics include document delivery, reference (both quick and extended), data base searching, and access to the building.

Document Delivery

There are two possible parts to this service which one could consider offering which are mutually exclusive: 1) loan of materials that the patron would return and, 2) photocopy or purchase of materials that the patron keeps forever. Obviously, one could decide to have one service without the other. When considering loan of books one could decide that it is too risky to loan books to individuals or corporations who are not associated with the academic community. The motivation for some people to return materials is not great and you cannot, for example, put a "hold-credit" on the XYZ Company. On the other extreme, one could decide not only to loan the books from the home institution but be willing to loan materials borrowed from another library. At MITS we have made the decision to lend books from our library but we will not borrow a book from another library to loan to one of our clients. In general our clients have been responsible and cooperative and only one book has been lost in almost two years of service.

Loaning books does not make up a large portion of our document delivery requests — only three percent of our document delivery requests are for books. Depending on your collection and the group of people you intend to serve, your figures could be quite different.

Photocopies of journal articles and other technical papers and reports make up the bulk of our document delivery. In many ways they are easier, philosophically, to provide. When a copy is made the material is not away from the shelf long and primary users of the collection are not denied access to it for several weeks. Once the photocopy is sent, the transaction is complete — one does not have to worry about books charged out or overdue notices. On the other hand, with photocopies there are copyright laws to worry about and one must be sure to have a signed statement from the patron accepting copyright responsibility or have complete records to make payments to the Copyright Clearance Center. The establishment of the Copyright Clearance Center and paying royalties was not something most people worried about ten years ago. From the client's point of view, copy or purchase of materials means that the client can do with it as he wishes and keep it as long as needed.

Interlibrary loan is a service that used to be provided to patrons free but it is becoming an issue because limited economic resources are facing most academic libraries today. For most publicly supported institutions there is the reality of fewer tax dollars going into the state budget, and education taking more than an "across the board" cut. These constant (or less than constant) dollars must maintain services and purchase library materials which continue to escalate in price. Obviously, the economic recession is straining the book budget and the same dollars purchase fewer materials than in years past. Coupled with this is an information explosion which means libraries are buying less of what is published. Not only is more material being published, but that material is being published in alternative formats: online sources, videodiscs, microforms, cassettes, computer tapes, and so on. The impact on interlibrary loan is twofold: first, the library is able to purchase fewer materials needed by their faculty and students for research and teaching. And secondly, union lists are seldom notified when libraries cancel serial subscriptions so the ILL staff must often try several locations for borrowed items. Each additional location which must be tried increases the cost of that transaction. It is also more costly for the library receiving the requests because they must check their holdings for serials which are no longer received.

The economic recession is also straining the staff. With fewer dollars in the budget, staff are not replaced when they leave. The remaining (smaller) staff must maintain or increase their work load.

The cumulative effect of more work with scarce economic resources is causing people to scrutinize their operations in a way that was never necessary in the past. Streamlining procedures is always useful but now people are often examining the mission statement of the institution and making distinctions about levels of service for various categories of users. Service to non-primary clientele can no longer be absorbed by the institutions.

Another environmental change affecting interlibrary loan is the increase in technology and library networks. We have developed shared cataloging systems such as OCLC and RLIN which makes libraries more aware of who has what. Larger demands are being placed on ILL offices because networking makes holdings better known. Smaller libraries have probably felt the impact most of all. With the advent of computer networks more people can ascertain that materials are held in a given library.

Access to the Library Building

Some major research libraries who used to have walk-in access are now considering assessing a fee for entering their building. This is a change. Usually people have to pay a fee to get into the *stacks* but Princeton, for example, now charges to get into the building. This impacts reference because if there is a fee to get into the building, there is also a charge for using reference. Some reasons an institution may take such actions are the following:

1) Scarcity of resources and intensity of use of the resources which are held. There are simply not enough copies of books to go around. If, for example, a library holds only two copies of a book and lets the "world" in, the library will need more than two copies to serve the clientele who need it for research or teaching.

2) Conservation and preservation of materials which are owned. There will be far less wear and tear on the collection with fewer clients using them.

3) Security from theft and mutilation of the materials and security of people (staff and patrons); with a controlled population the incidence of mutilation goes down.

4) Space for collections and for study. There is a real problem in many libraries to have enough physical space in the stacks for books and in the public areas for readers.

5) Complexity of library systems and management. There are many management considerations in opening up a library's clientele such as who will reshelve all the books that have been used which impacts both budget and staffing. Time spent on reference with outsiders also limits the reference and related services it is possible to provide for primary clientele.

In terms of access to the building I must comment that information brokers are part of the changing environment. Outside information brokers are mining research collections for their own use and making a profit from it. The problems of this occurrence are wear and tear on the collection, including bent pages, broken bindings, lost materials, and replacement of material more frequently because of increased use. There is also an increase in questions at the reference desk and an increase in reshelving of materials.

One has to question why a library would not prefer to set up its own information brokerage so that any profits could be returned to the general budget to help offset some of the additional costs which will occur anyway. The library staff can be trained in preservation techniques to be more careful than an outside user and will have an incentive to reshelve materials or take them to the sorting area. Information brokers making use of library collections for profit is reason enough to charge them for access to the building.

Reference

It is important to make a distinction between quick and extended reference questions. I believe that there are several problems with charging for quick reference not the least of which is administrability. And, for publicly supported institutions, I think it would be difficult to refuse to look up an address for the public.

Each library will have to decide for themselves when reference questions cease being quick and become extended questions, and therefore are candidates for fees. A general guideline I have suggested for librarians at the University of Michigan is fifteen minutes — plus or minus — in their professional judgment. In some cases, it may be reasonable to charge a department, faculty, or students for extended reference if the type of help they require is beyond that which can be provided for everyone on the campus. Where that point is, and if it exists at all, is something that each library will have to define for themselves employing both a philosophical position and practical considerations: even if you were willing to do extended reference for everyone, not everyone would ask. When charging for reference one needs to determine an hourly rate that will recover the necessary costs and if there will be a minimum charge assessed.

The definition of extended reference could include special expertise from the staff such as language skills, thorough knowledge of the collection, or command of the reference bibliography in a given subject. There are some specialized public services which libraries have never offered for their clientele in the past because they did not have the resources to do so. These include such services as indexing, translations, cataloging, compilation of a bibliography by hand, and lengthy research projects of various sorts. With a fee-based service it is possible to offer these in-depth, specialized services to an institution's faculty, students, and departments, as well as to outside groups. Since the costs of such specialized services will be recovered these services can be tailored to the requestors precise specifications. Extra staff can be hired to meet changing needs. The net effect is to enhance public services because it makes available extraordinary services which otherwise could not have been provided.

Online Search Services

Data base searching can be used for compiling a bibliography, searching for a fact, verifying a citation, and most of these activities are more highly specialized services than libraries have done in the past. A good way to look at charges for data bases is to make comparisons between what a library would be willing to provide manually and work out an equivalent measure of service for the data bases. For example, if you would not charge a patron to verify a citation manually and the most efficient way to do that verification is online, it makes sense to have the library absorb the cost of doing a quick reference search online. A good example of this situation is comparing a manual search through 36 uncumulated issues of *Government Report Announcements* or an online search in NTIS. Clearly one or two dollars of online time is less costly than 15 to 30 minutes of staff time. If a library sees reference data base searching as fundamental but has no increase in the budget to absorb this activity, then it must be prepared to reduce the support of another activity to make reference searching possible.

Compiling a bibliography is much more extensive and expensive an endeavor, either manually or online, and the chances are great that there will be a charge for this service in most libraries. Online search services differ from those services traditionally provided by libraries since they are: 1) relatively expensive, 2) have costs which are easily calculable, 3) are tailored to individual users with little value to others, and 4) direct charges are incurred each time an online search is conducted (versus a one time expenditure for a book).

Aside from the online computer time and offline prints one can charge for the librarian's expertise: ability to subdivide a question into its component parts, knowledge of the strengths and idiosyncrasies of each file, and familiarity with the computer vendor's system capabilities and shortcuts. Of course, part of this expertise is knowing when *not* to go online. Since data base searching is expensive, it seems reasonable for a library to pass along these costs to the individual(s) who benefit. In a recent American Library Association survey, Mary Jo Lynch found that 92 percent of 985 publicly supported libraries charge fees to some or all of those using their online search services (Lynch, 1982, p. 174).

MITS

The idea for MITS was developed about four years ago out of a committee which advises the director — The Advisory Group (TAG). The University Library was receiving many requests from outside users for document delivery and data base searching. These requestors needed the material quickly but we could only take their requests as received and put them in the pile with requests from faculty and students without priority. This was frustrating to both the staff and the outside clients. We were not recovering our full costs for staff time to complete data base requests, and as budget and people were cut back we had fewer staff to handle the regular demand let alone the requests from business and industry. There was general feeling that if an office could be set up to handle outside users it would serve the business community well by opening up the resources of the university to them and provide them with a fast service that would meet their needs. It would also relieve a burden on the U-M staff since they would no longer have to deal with reference questions, data base searches, and document delivery requests from business and industry. Since the mission of our university library is to serve faculty and students it was very important that the outside users office be totally cost recovery.

A proposal for MITS was drafted by a subcommittee and it was taken for approval to the appropriate units of the university. Following the decision to proceed with MITS, a job description was written and posted and I applied for the job. At that time I was the social sciences reference librarian and bibliographic instructor and was responsible for training all the other data base searchers on campus. It was very useful to be thoroughly familiar with reference, the campus library system, and data base searching. MITS was started with some seed money from a trust fund; thus, no tax dollars were involved.

MITS is not in competition with the regular staff but rather supplements existing reference services because we do projects that are larger than a university reference librarian can afford to spend time doing. We also serve a clientele that the university's librarian does not. MITS has done some work for university departments and faculty who had projects that were beyond the scope of what the university library could provide. For example, MITS proved to be quite useful last January after The University of Michigan Economics

Department burned to the ground and they needed help determining the cost of replacement journals for the insurance company. Most of our clients, however, are companies and over 500 businesses used MITS in the first year and a half. Sixty-six percent of the requests were from Michigan and thirty-four percent were from non-Michigan clients; and non-Michigan can mean Japan or Australia. MITS can be used by companies with libraries as a supplement to their holdings or as a safety valve – backup staff for illness or vacation. Small companies without corporate libraries use MITS in place of a library and only when needed.

The University of Michigan Library, with the fifth largest academic library collection in the United States, was well suited to have a fee based information service. Because we have a rich research collection with thousands of serials, research reports, government documents, and monographs we can fill most of our requests in-house. We also have access to two shared cataloging systems – OCLC and RLIN.

MITS serves all subject areas and offers a full range of services including document delivery, data base searching, in-depth research, and translations. Our document delivery requests are received through the mail, DIALORDER, ORBDOC, telephone, and TWX. Requests are filled within two working days if the items are in the University of Michigan collection and it is not necessary to "unscramble" the citation. Seventy-five percent of the document delivery requests are filled in-house. MITS will try to obtain the document from elsewhere if we do not have the needed item. While MITS offers in-depth reference we do not do quick reference – the reference desks in the various divisional libraries do that. If the question becomes very involved then the patron is referred to MITS. Conversely, if a patron calls MITS and all they really need is an address we will refer them to the appropriate reference desk and there is no charge.

I have had many reactions to our price schedule but, in general, librarians find us expensive and business people find us cheap. My own personal theory on the matter is that most librarians have not worked with a budget and do not know how expensive it really is to provide service. When you must recover the costs of the secretary, fringe benefits, paper clips, and telephone – to name a few – it is necessary to charge more than five cents per page for copying. Our invoices must reflect the cost of the staff time to gather the information plus the direct expenses incurred while doing so. Our patrons are paying for the expertise to know where to look, staff time, and speed – not for the information. MITS will spend as much time as is necessary and reasonable on a question as long as we have a client who is willing to have us go to those lengths.

The advertising and promotion of MITS has included speaking to local businesses, associations, and on the radio, direct mail, press releases from the U-M Information Services, and 30-second spot from ABC Sports, advertisements in newspapers and journals, and exhibit booths.

MITS is staffed with a full time librarian, secretary, student assistants to "go and fetch" and people with special expertise, like translators, are hired as needed. Because MITS is self supporting we have the ability to hire staff to meet changing needs.

If any of you are considering setting up a fee based information service in your library you should be aware of the tremendous commitment you are making. A dedicated staff is essential. If the staff has other responsibilities they will be put in an awkward position when they will inevitably have to balance the needs of the academic and business community. The priorities must be clear. It takes a lot of hard work to make an information brokerage successful: flexibility, creativity, and determination are required. There must also be a demonstrated need in your area for the service and it will require seed money to get started. Let me remind you that it is essentially a small business and the small business literature shows that it takes two to three years for a small business to break even — and they do not all make it. So, there are some risks involved.

MITS has served a real need at the University of Michigan Library. It has opened up our collections to outside users by making material from it available on a timely basis. Business and industry is very pleased and the staff is delighted to have some place to send the outside users.

BIBLIOGRAPHY

Becker, Joseph. "Libraries, Society, and Technological Change." *Library Trends*, 27 (Winter 1978), 409--416.

Blake, Fay M. and Jane Irby. "The Public Library and the Information Industry." *Drexel Library Quarterly*, 12 (January-April, 1976), 149--58.

Boss, Richard W. and Lorig Maranjian. *Fee-based Information Services; a Study of a Growing Industry*. New York: Bowker, 1980. (Information Management Series, 1.)

Boss, Richard. "The Library as an Information Broker." *College and Research Libraries*, 40 (May, 1979), 136--140.

Cooper, Michael. "Charging Users for Library Services." *Information Process and Management*, 14 (no. 6, 1978), 419--427.

DeGennaro, Richard. "Pay Libraries and User Charges." *Library Journal*, 100 (February 15, 1975), 363--367.

Dougherty, Richard M. "Fees and Subsidies." *Journal of Academic Librarianship*, 5 (July, 1979), 123.

Dougherty, Richard M. "Fees or Subsidies: A Revisionist View." *Journal of Academic Librarianship*, 6 (January, 1981), 323.

External User Services. Washington, DC: Systems and Procedures Exchange Center, Association of College and Research Libraries, Office of Management Studies, 1981. (SPEC flyer; April 1981, no. 73).

Fees for Services. Washington, DC: Systems and Procedures Exchange Center, Association of College and Research Libraries, Office of Management Studies, 1981. (SPEC flyer; May 1981, no. 74).

Felicetti, Barbara Whyte. "Information for Fee and Information for Free: The Information Broker and the Public Librarian." *Public Library Quarterly*, 1 (Spring, 1979), 9--20.

Finnigan, Georgia. "Nontraditional Information Services." *Special Libraries*, 67 (February 1976), 102--103.

Gell, Marilyn Killebrew. "User Fees I: The Economic Argument." *Library Journal*, 104 (January 1, 1979), 19--23.

Gell, Marilyn Killebrew. "User Fees II: The Library Response." *Library Journal*, 104 (January 15, 1979), 170--173.

Information Broker/Free Lance Librarians — New Careers — New Library Services Workshop. Syracuse, New York. *Proceedings*. Edited by Barbara B. Minor. Syracuse, NY: Syracuse University School of Information Studies, 1976. (Miscellaneous Studies, 3.)

Journal of Fee-based Information Services, I (January-February, 1979--).

King, Donald. "Pricing Policies in Academic Libraries." *Library Trends*, 27 (Summer, 1979), 47--62.

Kranich, Nancy. "Fees for Library Service: They Are Not Inevitable!" *Library Journal*, 105 (May 1, 1980), 1048–1051.

Linsley, Laurie S. "Academic Libraries in an Interlibrary Loan Network." *College and Research Libraries*, 43 (July, 1982), 292–299.

Lynch, Mary Jo. "Libraries Embrace Online Search Fees." *American Libraries*, 14 (March, 1982), 174.

Nitecki, Danuta A. "Online Services." *RQ*, 20 (Winter, 1980), 117–120.

Penner, Rudolf J. "The Practice of Charging Users for Information Services: A State of the Art Report." *Journal of the American Society for Information Science*, 21 (January-February, 1970), 67–74.

Rettig, James. "Rights, Resolutions, Fees, and Reality." *Library Journal*, 106 (February 1, 1981), 301–304.

Spencer, Louisa D. "Growing Demand for Information-to-Order." *Savvy*, 2 (January, 1981), 20–23.

Warnken, Kelly. *The Information Broker; How to Start and Operate Your Own Fee-based Service*. New York: Bowker, 1981. (Information Management Series, 2.)

Bibliography

Rodney M. Hersberger

The papers presented in this volume view the changing environment of reference services and the people who provide those services from several perspectives. Since all libraries offer reference and information services, there are many contributions to the literature on this topic. This selected bibliography attempts to propose readings and discussions to supplement the papers. To establish some time limitations, no items in the bibliography pre-date 1970. The bibliography is organized into seven categories to focus on the various themes represented in the volume.

GENERAL ISSUES AND DISCUSSIONS OF REFERENCE SERVICES

Aluri, R. "Academic Reference Librarians: An Endangered Species." *Journal of Academic Librarianship* 4:82--4. May 1978.

Blakely, F. "Perceiving Patterns of Reference Service: A Survey." *RQ* 11:30--8. Fall 1971.

Bunge, C.A. "Seekers vs Barriers; Getting Information to People: Your Role." *Wisconsin Library Bulletin* 70:76--8. March 1974.

Boucher, V. "Nonverbal Communication and the Library Reference Interview." *RQ* 16:27–32. Fall 1976.

"Eight Views of Reference." *RQ* 11:205–21. Spring 1972.

Emery, R. "Steps in Reference Theory." *Library Association Record* 72:88--90. March 1970.

Ferriero, D.S. "Burnout at the Reference Desk." *RQ* 21:274--79. Spring 1982.

Gothberg, H.M. "Communication Patterns in Library Reference and Information Service." *RQ* 13:7--14. Fall 1973.

Gothberg, H.M. "Immediacy: A Study of Communication Effect on the Reference Process." *Journal of Academic Librarianship* 2:126–9. July 1976.

Gration, S.U. "Reference Bibliographers in the College Library." *College & Research Libraries* 35:28--34. January 1974.

Holland, B. "Updating Library Reference Services through Training for Interpersonal Competence." *RQ* 17:207–11. Spring 1978.

Holler, F.L. "Toward a Reference Theory." *RQ* 14:301--9. Summer 1975.

Hunter, R.P. "Reference Service with a Patron Centered Approach." *Catholic Library World* 50:225--7. December 1978.

Jain, S.K. "3 R's of Reference Service." *RQ* 11:51--3. Fall 1971.

Jahoda, G. "Analyzing the Reference Process." *RQ* 12:148--56. Winter 1972.

Katz, W.H. *Introduction to Reference Work*. New York: McGraw-Hill, 1978.

King, G.B. "Open & Closed Reference Questions." *RQ* 12:157--60. Winter, 1972.

Lopez Munoz, J. "Significance of Non-Verbal Communication in the Reference Interview." *RQ* 16:220--4. Spring 1977.

McFadyen, D. "Psychology of Inquiry: Reference Service and the Concept of Information/Experience." *Journal of Librarianship* 7:2–11. January 1975.

McInnis, R.G. *New Perspectives for Reference Service in Academic Libraries*. Greenwood Press. 1978. 351p.

Neville, S.H. "Job Stress and Burnout: Occupational Hazards for Service Staff." *College and Research Libraries* 42(3):242--47. May 1981.

Reference and Information Services: A Reader. Ed. by W.A. Katz. Scarecrow Press, 1978. 456p.

ReHig, J. "Theoretical Model and Definition of the Reference Process." *RQ* 18:19–29. Fall 1978.

Rugh, A.G. "Toward a Science of Reference Work: Basic Concepts." *RQ* 14:293–9. Summer 1975.

St. Clair, J.W. "Staffing the Reference Desk: Professionals or Nonprofessionals?" *Journal of Academic Librarianship* 3:149–53. July 1977.

Shores, L. "Basic Reference: An Information Theory." *RQ* 13:199–205. Spring 1974.

Shores, L. *Reference as the Promotion of Free Inquiry.* Littleton, CO: Libraries Unlimited, 1976.

Slavens, T.P. *Informational Interviews and Questions.* Metuchen, NJ: Scarecrow Press, 1978.

Turner, S.W. "Relevant Reference Training." *PNLA Quarterly* 40:15–17. April 1976.

Vavrek, B.F. "Nature of Reference Librarianship." *RQ* 13:213–17. Spring 1974.

Vavrek, B.F. "Reference Service: Back to Basics." *Catholic Library World* 47:64–7. September 1975.

Whittaker, K. "Towards a Theory for Reference and Information Service." *Journal of Librarianship* 9:49–63. January 1977.

Wilkinson, J.P. "The Step Approach to Reference Service." *RQ* 17:293–300. Summer 1978.

REFERENCE SERVICES MEASUREMENT AND EVALUATION

Balay, R.E. "Use of the Reference Service in a Large Academic Library." *College & Research Libraries* 36:9–26. January 1975.

Bradenall, J. "Client Assessment of Reference Services." *Australian Library Journal* 25, no. 15:367–9. November 1976.

Childers, T.A. "Managing the Quality of Reference/Information Service." *Library Quarterly* 42:212--17. April 1972.

Childers, T.A. "Test of Reference." *Library Journal* 105:924–8. April 15, 1980.

Ellison, J.W. "Personal Accountability Form for Academic Reference Librarians: A Model." *RQ* 16:142--8. Winter 1976.

"Evaluation of Reference Sources and Reference Services." (In Katz, W.A. *Introduction to Reference Work: V. 2. Reference Services and Reference Processes.* 2d ed. McGraw-Hill, 1974. pp. 239--61.)

Gebhard, P. "Networking in the Microcosm; or Reference Referrals." *RQ* 17:197–201. Spring 1978.

Gothberg, H.M. "Communication Patterns in Library Reference and Information Services." *RQ* 13:7–14. Fall 1973.

Halldorsson, E.H. "Performance of Professionals and Nonprofessionals in the Reference Interview." *College & Research Libraries* 38:385–95. September 1977.

Halperin, M. "Measuring Students Preferences for Reference Service: A Conjoint Analysis." *Library Quarterly* 50:208--24. April 1980.

Horn, R.G. "Why They Don't Ask Questions." *RQ* 13:225--33. Spring 1974.

House, D.E. "Reference Efficiency or Reference Deficiency." *Library Association Record* 76:222–23. November 1974.

Howell, B.J. "Fleeting Encounters – A Role Analysis of Reference Librarian-Patron Interaction." *RQ* 16:124--9. Winter 1976.

Lancaster, F.W. *The Measurement and Evaluation of Library Services.* Washington: Information Resources Press, 1977.

Lopez, M.D. "Academic Reference Service: Measurement, Costs and Value." *RQ* 12:234--42. Spring 1973.

Morgan, C. "Reference Librarian's Need for Measures for Reference." *RQ* 14:11–13. Fall 1974.

Murfin, M.E. *Study of the Reference Process in a University Library.* 1970. 221p. Thesis, Kent State University.

Murphy, M. *Criteria and Methodology for Evaluating the Effectiveness of Information and Reference Services in Academic Libraries: A Regional Case Study.* Thesis (Ph.D.), University of Pittsburgh.

Myers, M.J. "The Accuracy of Telephone Reference Services in the Southeast: A State of the Art" in *Library Effectiveness: A State of the Art.* Chicago: LAMA, 1980. p. 220–33.

Nelson, J.A. "Faculty Awareness and Attitudes toward Academic Library Reference Services: A Measure of Communication." *College & Research Libraries* 34:268–75. September 1973.

Pings, V.M. "Reference Services Accountability and Measurement." *RQ* 16:120–3. Winter 1976.

Spicer, C.T. "Measuring Reference Service: A Look at the Cornell University Libraries Reference Question Recording System." *Bookmark* 31:79–81. January 1972.

Vavrek, B.J. "Reference Evaluation – What the 'Guidelines' Don't Indicate." *RQ* 18:335–40. Summer 1979.

White, H.D. "Measurement at the Reference Desk." *Drexel Library Quarterly* 17:3–35. Winter 1981.

White, R.W. "Measuring the Immeasurable: Reference Standards." *RQ* 11:308–10. Summer 1972.

INSTRUCTION IN LIBRARY USE

Beaubien, A.K. *Learning the Library: Concepts and Methods for Effective Bibliographic Instruction.* New York: Bowker, 1982.

Cooper, N.P. "Library Instruction at a University-Based Information Center: The Informative Interview." *RQ* 15:233–40. Spring 1976.

Cottam, K.M. "Avoiding Failure: Planning User Education." *RQ* 21:331–33. Summer 1982.

Dreifuss, R. "Library Instruction in the Database Searching Context." *RQ* 21:233–8. Spring 1982.

Eisenbach, E. "Bibliographic Instruction from the Other Side of the Desk." *RQ* 17:312–16. Summer 1978.

Griffin, L.W. "Orientation and Instruction of Graduate Students in the Use of the University Library: A Survey." *College & Research Libraries* 33:467–72. November 1972.

Hernon, P. "Floating Reference Librarian." *RQ* 12:60–4. Fall 1972.

Hicks, J.T. "Computer-Assisted Instruction in Library Orientation and Services." *Medical Library Association Bulletin* 64:238–40. April 1976.

Hopkins, F.L. "A Century of Bibliographic Instruction: The Historical Claim to Professional and Academic Legitimacy." *College & Research Libraries* 43(3):192–98. May 1982.

Knapp, S.D. "Instructing Library Patrons about Online Reference Services." *Bookmark* 38:237–42. Fall 1979.

Lubans, J., Jr. Ed. *Educating the Library User.* New York: Bowker, 1974.

Mignon, E. "Information Science in the Teaching of Traditional Reference Service." American Society for Information Science. Proceedings. 1971. pp. 143–6.

Murphy, M. "Reference/Advisory Interview: Its Contribution to Library-User Education." (In Lubans, J., ed. *Educating the Library User.* Bowker, 1974. pp. 287–306.)

Paterson, E.R. "Assessment of College Student Library Skills." *RQ* 17:226–9. Spring 1978.

Rader, H.B. "Reference Services as a Teaching Function." *Library Trends* 29:95–103. Summer 1980.

Rhodes, R.G. "Educational Role of the University Library and the Provision of Information Services." *IATUL Proceedings* 7:11–25. July 1973.

Starks, D.D. "Two Modes of Computer Assisted Instruction in a Library Reference Course." *Journal of the American Society for Information Science* 23:271–7. July 1972.

THE FEE QUESTION

Blake, F.M. "Libraries in the Marketplace: Information Emporium or People's University?" *Library Journal* 99:108–11. January 15, 1974.

Blake, F.M. "Rush to User Fees: Alternative Proposals." *Library Journal* 102:20005–8. October 1, 1977.

Becker, J. "Libraries, Society, and Technological Change." *Library Trends* 27:409–16. Winter 1978.

Boss, R.W. *Fee-Based Information Services; a Study of a Growing Industry.* New York: Bowker, 1980.

Charging for Computer-Based Reference Services; Proceedings of a Program Organized by MARS of RASD at the 1977 ALA Conference in Detroit. Ed. by P.G. Watson. ALA, RASD, 1978. 49p.

Cooper, M.D. "Charging Users for Library Service." *Information Processing and Management* 14(6): 419–27. 1978.

DeGennaro, R. "Pay Libraries and User Charges." *Library Journal* 100:363–7. February 15, 1975.

Dodd, J.B. "Pay-as-You-Go Plan for Satellite Industrial Libraries Using Academic Facilities." *Special Libraries* 65:66–72. February 1974.

Eshelman, W.R. "Pay Libraries: Can We Afford Them." *Wilson Library Bulletin* 50:680–2. May 1976.

Gell, M.K. "User Fees I: The Economic Argument." *Library Journal* 104:19–23. January 1979.

Gell, M.K. "User Fees II: The Library Response." *Library Journal* 104:170–73. January 15, 1979.

Huston, M.M. "Fee or Free: The Effect of Charging on Information Demand." *Library Journal* 104:1811–14. September 15, 1979.

King, D.W. "Pricing Policies in Academic Libraries." *Library Trends* 28:47–62. Summer 1979.

"Service to Business: The Fee Question." *Library Journal* 100:1182. June 15, 1975.

Watson, P.G. "Dilemma of Fees for Service: Issues and Actions for Librarians." In *ALA Yearbook*, p. xv–xxii. 1978.

White, H.S. "Who Pays for Peripheral Services, and What Are They Anyway?" *American Libraries* 13:40, 44. January 1982.

THE INFLUENCE OF COMPUTERS ON REFERENCE SERVICES

Artundi, S.A. "Man, Information and Society: New Patterns of Interaction." *Journal of the American Society for Information Science* 30:15–18. January 1979.

Barraclough, E.D. "On-Line Searching in Information Retrieval." *Journal of Documentation* 33:220–38. September 1977.

Bivins, K.T. "REFLES [Reference Library Enhancement System]: An Individual Microcomputer System for Fact Retrieval." *On-Line Review* 4:357–65. December 1980.

Cogswell, J.A. "On-Line Search Services: Implications for Libraries and Library Users." *College & Research Libraries* 39:275–80. July 1978.

Dolan, D.R. "The Quality Control of Search Analysts." *Online* 3:8–16. April 1979.

Ensor, P. "The Expanding Use of Computers in Reference Service." *RQ* 21:365–72. Summer 1982.

Gardner, T.A. "Effect of On-Line Data Bases on Reference Policy." *RQ* 19:70–4. Fall 1979.

Hoover, R.E. "Computer Aided Reference Services in the Academic Library; Experiences in Organizing and Operating an Online Reference Service." *Online* 3:28–41. October 1979.

Jahoda, G. "Reference Question Analysis and Search Strategy Development By Man and Machine." *Journal of the American Society for Information Science* 25:139--44. May 1974.

Kilgour, F.G. "Increased UAP (Universal Availability of Publications) Effected by an On-Line Catalogue." *Interlending Review* 7:20--2. January 1979.

Klugman, S. "Online Information Retrieval Interface with Traditional Reference Services." *On-Line Review* 4:263–70. September 1980.

Knapp, S.D. "Budgeting to Provide Computer-Based Reference Services: A Case Study." *Journal of Academic Librarianship* 5:9–13. March 1979.

Knapp, S.D. "Reference Interview in the Computer Based Setting." *RQ* 17:320--4. Summer 1978.

Maxwell, M.F. "Machine in the Reference Room." *RQ* 11:23--5. Fall 1971.

Robertson, S.E. "Theories and Models in Information Retrieval." *Journal of Documentation* 33:126--48. June 1977.

Warden, C.L. "Online Searching of Bibliographic Databases: The Role of the Search Intermediary." *Bookmark* 36:35--41. Winter 1977.

Wax, M. *A Handbook for the Introduction of On-Line Bibliographic Search Services into Academic Libraries.* Washington: Association of Research Libraries, Office of University Library Management Studies, 1976.

Winik, R. "Reference Function with an Online Catalog." *Special Librarian* 63:217--21. May-June 1972.

PROFESSIONALISM IN LIBRARIANSHIP

Abell, M.D. "The Changing Role of the Academic Librarian: Drift and Mastery." *College & Research Libraries* 40(2):154--164. March 1979.

Asheim, L.E. "Librarians as Professionals." *Library Trends* 27: 225–57. Winter 1979.

Cameron, D.B. "Credentials Question: Why We Care." *Journal of Academic Librarianship* 5:83–5. May 1979.

Cottam, K.M. "Interviewing for Employee Selection." *Tennessee Librarian* 31:33–5. Fall 1979.

Cottam, K.M. "Minimum Qualifications and the Law: The Issue Ticks Away for Librarians." *American Libraries* 11:280–1. May 1980.

Crickman, R.D. "Emerging Information Professional." *Library Trends* 23:311–27. Fall 1979.

Duncan, C.B. *Analysis of Tasks Performed by Reference Personnel in College and in University Libraries.* Thesis (Ph.D.) Indiana University. 1974.

Erlich, M. "Unprofessionalism in Librarianship." *Catholic Library World* 49:441–4. May 1978.

Flanagan, L.N. "Enemy Within, the Enemy Without; Two Major Impediments to the Development of Librarianship as a Profession." *Catholic Library World* 50: 171–6. November 1978.

Flanagan, L.N. "Professionalism Dismissed?" *College & Research Libraries* 34:209–14. May 1973.

Galloway, R.D. "Status or Stasis: Academic Librarian 10 Years Later." *American Libraries* 10:349–52. June 1979.

Giuliano, V.E. "Manifesto for Librarians." *Library Journal* 104: 1837–42. September 15, 1979.

Hanks, G. "An Alternative Model of a Profession for Librarians." *College & Research Libraries* 36(3): 175–187. May 1975.

Hauptman, R. "Professionalism or Culpability?" *Wilson Library Bulletin* 50:626–7. April 1976.

Hoffman, E.J. "Reference Librarians and Performance Appraisal." (In *Reference Interview*. Canadian Library Assn. n.d.p. 108–16.)

King. J.B. "What Future, Reference Librarian?" *RQ* 10:243–7. Spring 1971.

Koehler, B. "Professionalism: The Heart of the Matter." *Catholic Library World* 51:291–5. February 1980.

Nelson, B.R. "Chimera of Professionalism." *Library Journal* 105: 2029–33. October 1, 1980.

"Professionalism – An LJ Mini-Symposium." *Library Journal* 102: 1715–31. September 1, 1977.

Reeves, W.J. *Librarians as Professionals*. Lexington, MA: D.C. Heath. 1980.

Thomas, D.M. *The Effective Reference Librarian*. New York: Academic Press, 1981.

Vavrek, B.F. "Ethics for Reference Librarians." *RQ* 12:56–8. Fall 1972.

Wilson, P. "Professionalism under Attack!" *Journal of Academic Librarianship* 7:283–290. November 1981.

RESOURCE SHARING AND COLLECTION DEVELOPMENT: IMPACTS ON REFERENCE SERVICES

Choldin, M.T. "Resources for Cooperative Reference: The University of Illinois Slavic Reference Services as a Model." *RQ* 21:34–9. Fall 1981.

"Cooperative Reference: Hazards, Rewards, Prospects." *RQ* 18:355–68. Summer 1979.

DeGennaro, R. "Austerity, Technology and Resource Sharing: Research Libraries Face the Future." *Library Journal* 100:917–23. May 15, 1975.

DeGennaro, R. "Libraries and Networks in Transition: Problems and Prospects for 1980's." *Library Journal* 106:1045–9. May 15, 1981.

DeGennaro, R. "Resource Sharing in a Network Environment." *Library Journal* 105:353–5. February 1, 1980.

Edelman, H. "The Development of Collections in American University Libraries." *College & Research Libraries* 37(3):222–245. May 1976.

Gribben, J.H. "Interlibrary Cooperation and Collection Building." (In *Academic Library: Essays in Honor of Guy R. Lyle*. Scarecrow, 1974. pp. 105–17.)

Job, S. "Cooperative Reference and the Small Academic Library." *RQ* 17:325–7. Summer 1978.

Kochen, M. "Referential Consulting Networks." (In *Toward a Theory of Librarianship*. Scarecrow, 1973. pp. 187–220.)

Lynch, B.P. "Networks and Other Cooperative Enterprises: Their Effect on the Function of Reference." *RQ* 16:197–202. Spring 1976.

Quick, R.C. "Coordination of Collection Building by Academic Libraries." (In Josey, E.D., ed. *New Dimensions for Academic Library Service*. Scarecrow, 1975. pp. 100–20.)

Rothstein, S. "The Extended Library and the Dedicated Library: A Sceptical Outsider Looks at Union Catalogues and Bibliographic Networks." *Cataloguing and Classification Quarterly* 2(1/2):103–120.

Weber, D.C. "A Century of Cooperative Programs among Academic Libraries." *College and Research Libraries* 37(3):205–221. May 1976.

Wright, T.C. "Cooperative Reference Services Committee Program." *Library of Congress Information Bulletin* 37:517. August 25, 1978.

INDEX

AACR2   38, 67
ABI/INFORM   102
Abell, Millicent   49
Abstract(s)   3, 102
Academic library(ies)   3, 17, 18, 19, 20, 21, 23, 24, 25, 27, 28, 29, 39, 79, 85, 88, 95, 99, 102, 104, 109
Acquisition(s)   2, 28, 39, 40, 42, 65, 69, 71, 72
Administration   25, 26, 79, 101
American Libraries   23, 38, 41, 50
American Library Association   50, 54, 108
American Library Association. Library Instruction Round Table   4
American Library Association. Office for Library Personnel Resources   51, 52
American Library Association. Reference and Adult Services Division   1
American Library Association. Resources and Technical Services Division. Cataloging and Classification Section. Heads of Cataloging Departments Discussion Group   36
Ash Lee,   73

Asheim, Lester   49
Aspnes, Grieg   18
Associated College of the Midwest   74
Association of College and Research Libraries. Bibliographic Instruction Section   5
Association of Research Libraries   33, 34, 36
Automation   32, 34, 42

BRS   81, 85
Baker, Betsy   33
Battin, Patricia   54
Bibliographer(s)   18, 38, 39, 40, 41, 42, 84
Bibliographic instruction   5, 6, 17, 39, 79, 82, 83, 85, 86
Bibliographic utility   33, 66, 85
Bibliography(ies)   2, 3, 29, 43, 66, 75, 85, 106, 107
Bone, Larry   56, 57
Book(s)   4, 6, 11, 19, 23, 27, 30, 35, 36, 38, 41, 48, 50, 55, 66, 67, 69, 70, 71, 87, 103, 104, 105
Branch librarians   18, 19
Branch libraries   2
Brigham Young University   56

125

British Lending Library Division 71
Budget(s) 13, 21, 23, 24, 25, 26, 27, 28, 30, 46, 70, 71, 74, 90, 99, 100, 104, 105, 106, 107, 108, 109
Burchinal, Lee 29

California Academic Libraries List of Serials 68
Carnegie, Dale 48
Catalog(s) 2, 9, 29, 32, 33, 34, 37, 41, 42, 66, 67, 68, 69, 75, 85, 86
Cataloger(s) 34, 35, 36, 38, 42, 43
Cataloging 3, 20, 22, 31, 32, 33, 34, 36, 37, 38, 39, 40, 41, 42, 43, 64, 67, 74, 101, 105, 109
Center for Research Libraries 65, 71
Choice 40
Chronicle of Higher Education 20, 28, 80
Circulation 23, 24, 31, 32, 33, 37, 38, 40, 41
Collection development 2, 3, 23, 31, 33, 39, 41, 64, 65, 66, 70, 71, 73, 75, 84
Collection management 39
Columbia University 3, 56
Computer(s) 1, 5, 9, 10, 11, 12, 13, 23, 66, 68, 69, 74, 79, 81, 82, 83, 84, 85, 87, 100, 102, 104, 105, 107
Congressional Information System 102
Cooperative reference 9, 10
Copyright Clearance Center 104
Council on Library Resources 20, 71
Cutter, Charles 68

Database searching 10, 11, 13, 22, 31, 35, 38, 81, 82, 83, 99, 103, 107, 108, 109
Davinson, Donald 31
DeGennaro, Richard 67
Dewey, Melville 3
Dialog 22, 81, 85
Directory of Library Networks and Cooperative Library Organizations, 1980 69
Duke University 65

ERIC 34, 40
Economic 21, 90, 91, 104
Evaluation 47, 48, 57, 79, 85, 89, 90, 91, 92, 94, 96

Faculty 3, 17, 18, 19, 20, 21, 22, 23, 24, 25, 27, 28, 29, 35, 41, 49, 55, 58, 80, 84, 91, 100, 102, 104, 106, 107, 108
Fairthorne, Robert 20
Farmington Plan 65
Fees 13, 22, 80, 99, 100, 101, 102, 103, 105, 106, 108, 109, 110
Ferriero, David 86
Frost, Robert 53
Funding 23, 74

Gore, Daniel 65
Gorman, Michael 37, 38, 39
Government publications 31, 38, 40
Green, Samuel 2, 4

Hanks, Gardiner 49
Herzberg, Frederick 48
Hill, Napoleon 48
Hopkins, Coda 56
Hopkins, Frances 5
House, David 37

Index   102
Indexes and abstracts   37
Indexing   11, 22, 31, 87, 107
Information   1, 2, 3, 4, 5, 7, 8, 9, 10, 11, 12, 13, 20, 21, 25, 26, 27, 29, 31, 32, 50, 52, 64, 65, 66, 68, 69, 70, 71, 73, 74, 75, 80, 84, 85, 86, 87, 95, 99, 100, 101, 102, 104, 106, 109, 110
Information and referral services   9, 11, 12
Information desk   3
Interlibrary loan   3, 10, 25, 26, 31, 38, 64, 65, 69, 89, 101, 104, 105

Jahoda, Gerald   1
Jewett, Charles   2
Joeckel, Carlton   69
Journal   20, 21, 30, 55, 72, 103, 109, 110
Journal of Academic Librarianship   21, 49

Kaplan, Louis   2
Katz, William   1, 31
Kranich, Nancy   101

LJ Hotline   80
Ladd   28
Librarian(s)   2, 3, 4, 5, 6, 7, 8, 9, 10, 11, 17, 18, 20, 23, 27, 28, 29, 30, 31, 32, 34, 35, 37, 38, 42, 43, 48, 49, 50, 51, 52, 54, 55, 56, 57, 58, 64, 65, 67, 74, 79, 80, 81, 83, 84, 85, 86, 87, 90, 94, 95, 96, 106, 107, 108, 109, 110
Librarianship   2, 4, 5, 6, 20, 41, 42, 52, 54
Library administrators   20, 32, 63, 87

Library Control System   32
Library instruction   1, 2, 4, 5, 12, 31, 38, 42, 43, 57, 83, 84, 85, 87
Library Journal   51, 64, 67
Library of Congress   20, 67
Library of Congress Subject Headings   38
Library orientation   5
Library resources   5
Library schools   17, 42, 43, 51, 69, 84, 93
Library service   2, 9, 12, 18, 63, 79
Library Trends   49
Literature search   2, 3, 68
Longstreet, Christine   56
Lynch, Mary Jo   108

MARC   67
MEDLARS   22
MEDLINE   34
MELVYL   68
METRO   69
McBurney, Margot   54
McClelland, David   48, 51
Malonconico, S. Michael   68
Maltz, Maxwell   48
Management   21, 24, 25, 35, 39, 54, 105
Mandino, Og   48
Martin, Lowell   64, 75
Martin, Murrey   37, 38
Maslow, Abraham   48
Massachusetts Institute of Technology   22
Material(s)   2, 3, 4, 6, 7, 8, 9, 17, 18, 19, 21, 23, 24, 26, 27, 30, 38, 39, 42, 68, 71, 75, 100, 101, 103, 104, 105
Measurement   89, 91, 92, 93, 94, 95, 96
Michigan Information Transfer Source   99, 103, 108, 109, 110

Microform(s)   27, 68, 70, 71, 85, 104
Minnesota Union List of Serials   68
Monograph(s)   70, 109
Monroe, Margaret E.   1, 2, 4
Myer, Paul   48

NASA Information Facility   22
Nash, Herbert   65
National Endowment for the Humanities   103
National Library of Medicine   22
National Periodicals Center   71
National Science Foundation   103
National Science Foundation. Office of Science Information Services   29
National Technical Information Service   107
National Union Catalog   64
Network(s)   63, 65, 69, 70, 74, 104, 105
Neville, Sandra   86
New England Depository Library   65

OCLC   33, 40, 41, 43, 65, 67, 68, 69, 72, 85, 89, 105, 109
OnLine   24, 26, 27, 29, 40, 54, 67, 68, 69, 85, 86, 100, 101, 102, 104, 107, 108
Organization   2, 18, 24, 50, 54, 57, 81
Osburn, Charles   19

Periodical(s)   23, 72
Photocopy   24, 100, 103, 104, 109
Poole, William F.   2

Princeton University   64, 105
Project INTREX   22
Psychological Abstracts   102
Public library(ies)   2, 3, 4, 6, 7, 11, 17, 36, 69, 95
Public service(s)   25, 28, 32, 33, 41, 43, 54, 75, 79, 80, 82, 84, 85, 86, 99, 101, 107
Publishing   21

RLIN   33, 41, 67, 68, 72, 85, 89, 105, 109
RTSD Newsletter   32
Reader(s)   2, 3, 6, 39, 94, 105
Rees, Alan   1
Reeves, William   49
Reference collection   41
Reference department   3, 27, 33, 34, 35, 39, 40, 79, 85, 87, 89
Reference interview   6, 9, 10, 11, 55
Reference librarians   1, 8, 9, 10, 12, 13, 26, 27, 31, 32, 33, 34, 35, 36, 37, 38, 39, 40, 41, 42, 43, 55, 57, 63, 66, 67, 73, 79, 80, 82, 83, 84, 85, 87, 95, 101
Reference staff   3, 6, 12, 67, 79, 80, 83, 85, 87, 89, 94, 95
Reference theory   1, 2
Research   18, 20, 26, 28, 54, 55, 71, 72, 93, 95, 101, 102, 104, 105, 106, 107, 109
Research Libraries Group   65, 73
Research library   54, 71, 73, 74, 75, 105
Resource sharing   12, 63, 64, 65, 66, 68, 73, 74, 75
Rothstein, Samuel   2, 3

128

Rowell, Joseph 64, 65

SDC 81, 85
Schwartz, David 48
Search strategy 5. 9, 11, 22, 82, 90, 101
Selective dissemination of information 8, 29
Serial(s) 27, 66, 70, 71, 72, 104, 109
Sheehy, Eugene 56, 57, 59
Shera, Jesse 1
Special library(ies) 3, 4, 9, 17, 18, 19, 20, 22, 27, 28, 39
Spicer, Carolyn 56
Staffing 20, 69, 105
Stanford University 65, 70, 71, 72
Stone, Elizabeth 54
Student(s) 3, 5, 17, 18, 19, 23, 24, 25, 35, 41, 42, 43, 47, 55, 80, 84, 91, 93, 100, 101, 102, 104, 106, 107, 108, 110
Subject specialists 3, 18, 40
SUNY, Albany 27
Swanson, Patricia 10, 56
System(s) 21, 22, 42, 43, 50, 89, 90, 91, 105, 108, 109

Technical services 28, 31, 32, 33, 34, 36, 37, 38, 41, 42, 43
Technical process(ing) 24, 37, 39, 67
Technology 7, 10, 22, 33, 74, 100, 104
Thomas, Diana 32

Union List of Serials 64
United States Department of Education 52
United States Office of Personnel Management 52

Universal Serial and Book Exchange 41, 65
University(ies) 4, 24, 25, 27, 28, 33, 35, 36, 42, 57, 65, 88, 90, 93, 99, 102, 108
University library(ies) 3, 5, 32, 33, 34, 35, 37, 39, 72, 108
University of California 68
University of California. Berkeley 64, 67, 69, 70, 71, 72
University of California. Davis 70
University of Florida 72
University of Illinois 32, 69
University of Michigan 99, 106, 108, 109, 110
University of North Carolina 65
User 1, 2, 4, 5, 6, 9, 10, 11, 12, 13, 17, 18, 22, 26, 28, 31, 32, 37, 63, 67, 68, 72, 73, 75, 80, 81, 82, 83, 85, 86, 87, 91, 94, 100, 101, 102, 103, 107

Vosper, Robert 20

Wagers, Robert 1
Washington Library Network 32, 41
Watterson, George 2
Weber, David 64, 65
Wiggins, Marvin 55, 57
Wilson Library Bulletin 68
Wilson, Pauline 49
Winchell, Constance 56

Yeats, W.B. 63